KU-007-347

The Language of
DECEPTION

Oli

The Language of
DECEPTION
A Discourse Analytical Study

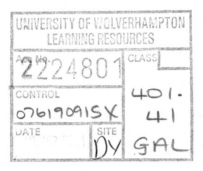

UNIVERSITY OF WOLVERHAMPTON
LEARNING RESOURCES

Acc No. 2224801   CLASS

CONTROL
076190915X

DATE   SITE DY

401.
41
GAL

DARIUSZ GALASIŃSKI

Sage Publications, Inc.
International Educational and Professional Publisher
Thousand Oaks ■ London ■ New Delhi

Copyright © 2000 by Sage Publications, Inc.

All rights reserved. No part of this book may be reproduced or utilized in any form or by any means, electronic or mechanical, including photocopying, recording, or by any information storage and retrieval system, without permission in writing from the publisher.

For information:

Sage Publications, Inc.
2455 Teller Road
Thousand Oaks, California 91320
E-mail: order@sagepub.com

Sage Publications Ltd.
6 Bonhill Street
London EC2A 4PU
United Kingdom

Sage Publications India Pvt. Ltd.
M-32 Market
Greater Kailash I
New Delhi 110 048 India

Printed in the United States of America

Library of Congress Cataloging-in-Publication Data

Galasiński, Dariusz.
   The language of deception: A discourse analytical study / by Dariusz Galasiński.
      p.   cm.
   Includes bibliographical references (p.   ) and index.
   ISBN 0-7619-0915-X (cloth: acid-free paper)
   1. Discourse analysis.   2. Deception.   I. Title.
   P302 .G338   2000
   401′.41—dc21   00-008039

This book is printed on acid-free paper.

00   01   02   03   04   05   06   7   6   5   4   3   2   1

Acquiring Editor:	Margaret H. Seawell
Editorial Assistant:	Sandra Krumholz
Production Editor:	Astrid Virding
Editorial Assistant:	Cindy Bear
Typesetter:	Lynn Miyata
Cover Designer:	Teri Greenberg

Contents

Introduction

Trust Me, I'm a Doctor is a title of a BBC program in which a general practitioner doctor tells his viewers all sorts of interesting things about how to keep healthy and how to avoid doing unhealthy things, as well as trying to get people more rational and better informed in their approach to medicine. One night, however, we learned that there was this man who was not a doctor but practiced medicine. He was not a doctor but prescribed medication. He was not a doctor but worked in a hospital. For a number of years, he managed to deceive not only his patients but also his colleagues—nurses and other physicians. His deception was found out by his own greed—he wanted to be registered with professional bodies, and they could not find the required documentation. If it had not been for this, he could have carried on "treating" people until today. He could have even become my doctor. This thought was disturbing enough for me to ask myself a question: How can I simply trust my doctor? What if she . . . I do not even want to think about it, especially when she prescribes medication to my children. This was an insight into the world of adults.

My son used to have a favorite book that he often wanted to be read before he went to bed. It contains 22 tales written by the brothers Grimm and adapted for young children. One evening, I was once again reading a story from the book, and it struck me that the narrative was based solely on the characters' duplicity and lying. I finished the story, put my son to bed, and took the book with me. It took me just over an hour to read all 22 stories. What I found was quite distressing: sisters lying about who they are, an innkeeper lying about what he did, Tom Thumb lying that he is going to help, kings making false promises, ladies-in-waiting assuming false identities, princesses asking servants to assume false identities—the instances were legion. Of the 22 tales in my son's book, only two (*sic!*) did not involve any type of deception. All others varied from containing some deception to having deception all along. Yes, yes, they were all punished, or lied for a good cause, but the world of the tales—well, would it simply mirror our own? That was an insight into the world of children.

Another insight into our adult world came again from the BBC. This time, Angus Deayton, one of the most popular and intelligent presenters today, investigated deception in the world around us. The results? No, we all are not people getting married just to get the bride's or the groom's money, or professional con persons living on others' credulousness. We do not even normally say we are sailors when we are nurses or bricklayers; we are not art dealers selling forgeries, we are not even spies. But, asked Deayton, what about the odd piece of stationery taken for private use, what about private telephone calls from work, and what about those *slightly* modified expenses claims? And job applications? Whichever way we look, we live surrounded by lies, half-truths, exaggerations, and slightly enhanced—almost truthful—accounts. And, in all honesty, these lies, damned lies, and job applications are not only theirs, as we might be tempted to think or even claim, but also ours.

This book is about what commonly surrounds us, what we have learned to live with and practice just about every day of our lives. This book is about how people—or shall I say *we*—try to deceive each other. I shall not, however, be interested here in all deception in all its forms. First, I shall concentrate on how we deceive each other using language, rather than any other means of communication. Deception always involves some sort of communicative situation and a message passed from the deceiver to the target. Here I shall be interested in how it is done when people talk to each other. Only toward the end of the book shall I be interested in the deceptive workings of photography. In such a way, I shall attempt to make a bridge between visual and linguistic deception.

Second, I shall narrow the focus of the book even further. I shall be interested in talking in the public domain—not only because the sphere of the political is normally thought to be conducive to such research but also because of the ease with which readers will see the patterns of communication they have experienced daily on television or the radio. In such a way, reading the book will literally be reading about what we know but rarely stop to think more carefully about.

Third, the book is not about those who deceive, or try to deceive; nor is it about those who are the target of such actions. Instead, it is about the message itself. In other words, I shall focus here on the means of deception. This does not mean, however, that the book is written with the aim of becoming a handy textbook on how to be a good liar. Rather, I am interested in the workings of the deceptive message, in how language can and is used to deceive others: What devices are used, and what resources does language offer?

OVERVIEW

Chapter 1 starts with the proposition that human communication is predominantly underpinned by a "truth bias," an assumption that language users will normally tell and expect to be told the truth. Yet the truth bias is juxtaposed with an abundance of deceptive practices in nearly every corner of our lives, both public and private. I discuss the operation of deception in three main areas: public, interpersonal relationships, and cultural traditions. In the first, I focus primarily on politics and bureaucracy; in the third, on (military) history and popular culture. In my discussion of attitudes toward deception, I point out that although our attitudes toward deception are negative, we not only deceive others but also think that others deceive us. The chapter is rounded off by a brief look at the role of deception in the forming of language—the very essence of humanity.

Chapter 2 critically examines the ways in which deception has been conceptualized by social scientists, with the main focus on communication studies. Both definitional and typological problems are dealt with. In the former case, it is proposed that the approach toward the definition of deception that withstands evidence is to define it as a type of manipulation—more specifically, manipulation of truth and falsity of utterances. In the latter case, a review of a number of typologies of the deceptive message leads to a conclusion that one of their major flaws is that they do not appear to be based on a clear set of criteria generating the typology. Finally, three theories of deceptive communication (interpersonal deception theory; propositional communication approach, and information manipulation theory) are critically examined. The discussion leads to the conclusion that the Gricean framework seems to be a useful means of conceptualizing communicative deception.

Chapter 3 is pivotal to the approach to deception that I advocate in the book. In the chapter, I first deal with one of the major problems facing a researcher of deceptive communication: the problem of ascertaining the deceptive intention in a natural context, as well as that of having access to the misrepresented reality. The solution to the problem of studying deception in its natural context can be solved by basing the study on debates and focusing on how debaters misrepresent others' contributions. In such a way, one achieves access both to the deceptive message and to the reality it refers to, alleviating in such a way also the problem of classifying the message as deceptive. This leads to the necessary focus on misrepresentation as the only empirically accessible facet of deception. One could argue, however, that misrepresentation is the most typical of types of deception.

In Chapter 3, I offer two aspects of the linguistic message as the basis for a typology of deception: (a) propositional content and (b) the utterance's function. Falsifications and distortions are categories generated by the former aspect; taking words out of context is a type of deceptive message related to the latter. I also argue that there is no reason to propose a new category for those deceptions that are attempted through the implicit part of the utterance. False presuppositions or implicatures still can be analyzed within the proposed typology. Implicit deception, however, is different from explicit deception in the sense that removing the deceptive information to the implied is a means of concealing it.

Chapter 4—in part based on an earlier article (Galasiński, 1996a)—focuses on evasion as a deceptive category: It asks the question of the nature of evasion's deceptiveness. In the chapter, I propose that it is not the falsity of a statement used by the speaker to evade the question that constitutes deceptiveness of an evasive act. Evasion is deceptive as an attempt to induce in the addressee a false belief as to the relevance of the answer. An evasive speaker therefore deceives the addressee insofar as her or his own utterance is concerned. Deceptiveness of evasion, therefore, is metadiscursive.

Chapter 5—which draws on my earlier analyses (Galasiński, 1996b, 1998)—takes up the notion of metadiscursive deception and discusses it in detail. Metadiscursive strategies of deception are aimed at concealing uncooperativeness of the utterance of which they are part. I argue that there are two main types of metadiscursive deception: strategies that aim to misrepresent the function of the utterance and those that attempt to show the propositional content of the utterance as cooperative. The former category includes masking actions—more particularly, I analyze means of concealing evasion and attack; in the latter, I deal with problems of implicit deceptions and manipulations of felicity conditions of speech acts. I also argue that the category of metadiscursive deception is useful in explaining deceptiveness of speech acts to which it is impossible to ascribe truth or falsity: Although neither true nor false, questions, promises, and commands can be deceptive. By presupposing something or by being insincere, they are deceptive metadiscursively. Finally, I also argue that the distinction within deceptive acts with regard to the object of deception (that aimed at the extralinguistic reality and that aimed at the utterance itself) enables incorporating deceptive communication into a general theory of deception.

Chapter 6 shows that deception may be an act of a single communicator but that it can also be a joint conversational endeavor. The chapter examines acts of misrepresentation as acts of cooperation. The analysis of a televised interview shows that its overall aim could not have been attained unless both speakers cooperated in making and accepting misrepresentations. Cooperation to misrepresent was also shown as cooperation to be uncooperative toward the onlooking audience.

Chapter 7 draws together the discussions of extralinguistic and metadiscursive deception. It is an attempt to sketch the pragmatics of deception: I ask questions of the communicative functions of deceptive utterances. The objective of this chapter is to lay out the foundations of the pragmatic description of deceptive communication, first on the basis of reference to lying and evasion. I argue that neither of the deceptive acts can be thought of as a type of speech act (with a distinct force, conventional goal, and propositional content). Lies are statements that are mendacious; evasiveness is an attribute of an utterance used as an answer. Evasive speakers are shown either to make their response safe or to waive any responsibility for the claim made. Finally, I propose to analyze deceptive communication as pragmatic acts (see Mey, 1993): nonovert acts of communication that rely on the performance of another act, one that appears to be cooperative.

The concluding chapter not only summarizes the main arguments of the book but also takes a brief look at deception by visual communication, more particularly, problems of deceptiveness of photography. I argue that the broad framework of deception in language—and particularly the distinction between extralinguistic deception and its metadiscursive counterpart—seems also to work with regard to visual communication, or at least an aspect of it. This, it seems to me, is probably the most exciting prospect of further research into the deceptive message from the view of linguistics in particular and communication studies in general. Such research would deal with multimodality of deception and the relationships between the various modes.

Acknowledgments

This book owes its existence to a number of people who helped or supported me when I was designing and writing it. To give justice and thank all of them would be impossible; I would like, however, to acknowledge my indebtedness to Bob Sanders, Peter Robinson, Karen Tracy, Tim Levine, and Mark Hamilton, for discussions and help at various stages of the work. I owe Howard Giles the moment in a lift in Chicago.

I owe the most to two persons, though. First, I would like to thank Aleksandra Galasińska, my "in-house" linguist and anthropologist whose readiness to talk deception with me went far beyond marital duties. Second, without the extensive comments and encouragement of Ulrike H. Meinhof, this book would certainly not be what it is, if it were at all. I would also like to thank Michal and Ania for understanding that they could not have access to the computer at all times.

My thanks also go to Margaret Seawell from Sage for two things: first, for our conversation in San Francisco, and, second, for believing in this book.

Finally, I would like to thank Paul Willis for his great support at my university.

Needless to say, all the book's shortcomings are my own.

The Natural Way of Being

TRUTH BIAS

Thou shalt not bear false witness against thy neighbor. Even if one believes Mark Twain (quoted in Barnes, 1994) that the eighth commandment forbids only one type of lie and not deception in general, the commandment is one of the fundamental principles underlying the everyday practice in the so-called Western world. We all know that lying is bad and telling the truth is good. Despite the occasional hesitation—should a doctor tell her or his patient about cancer?—our children, from their childhood, in their nursery rhymes (see Aitchison, 1996) and fairy tales, are taught that lying is bad and that being truthful is *the* way to conduct themselves. Moreover, just as we normally assume that there is a single reality, that things are one way or the other (Bilmes, n.d.), and thus that telling the truth should always be possible, we also normally assume that truthfulness and morality go together in a simple and uncomplicated way (Zagorin, 1990).

In addition, public life is full of examples of claims of truthfulness and condemnation of the opposite. In 1998, the Western media were saturated with political drama that centered on whether the president of the United States did or did not lie. BBC television's "Review of the Year" in December of that year presented the investigation of the independent counsel, Kenneth Starr, into the allegations that President Clinton lied under oath that he did not have a sexual relationship with Monica Lewinsky not as a subject concerning matters of the state but as a question of whether someone lied and was right or wrong to do that. The problems of President Clinton's conduct were encapsulated in one of his notorious rhetorical questions of what the meaning of *is* is. The *voces populi* presented in the program were asked to comment on the license of a public figure to lie when faced with accusations of an extramarital affair. The entire constitutional crisis and public life of the most powerful country in the world seem to have hovered around one single issue: deception.

In the 1995 Polish presidential elections, the fact that the victorious candidate concealed certain facts about his education gave rise to a surge of protests with the finale of the case in the Polish Supreme Court. In the popular belief, one who lies is not fit to be president. Accusations of sleaze in British politics led to setting up commissions or committees (the Nolan committee, for example) to show that the political leaders, and indeed the party echelons at large, are only too willing to be subjected to scrutiny and tested for their truthfulness and honesty and integrity. Finally, the recent imprisonment of Jonathan Aitken, former member of the British Cabinet, for perjury and obstruction of the cause of justice started off as a televised claim of the politician's truthfulness. The claim to truth is at the same time the claim to morality.

The all-importance of truth and truthfulness can also be seen from a different perspective, one not based on the high grounds of morality. In everyday life, truth is what one normally expects from the other. When we ask the time or the way, when we tell our names in an office, and in a myriad of other everyday situations, we never even stop to think whether what we are told is true. We take it for granted. All such interactions have made us acquire our truth bias (Buller & Burgoon, 1996b; Miller & Stiff, 1993; Robinson, 1996; cf. also Lieberman, 1977; Nyberg, 1993). As Robinson (1996) puts it, others' statements will be taken to be true and to mean what they appear to mean. He adds that any other assumption in communication would not make sense.

Indeed, Lewis (1969) sees truthfulness as convention crucially underpinning the ability to communicate. Bok (1978) describes it as a precondition of action and choice, the very fabric of a society. Similarly, in his theory of the cooperative principle that underlies any conversation, or, more generally, any communicative exchange, Grice (1975, 1989) proposes that alongside quantity, relation, and manner, the maxim of quality—referring to the truthfulness of one's utterance—forms part of what it takes to be a cooperative speaker. To communicate cooperatively, an interlocutor must be truthful. The idea is also seconded in the work of Habermas (1979; also 1987), who makes both truth and truthfulness two of the validity claims that are raised or presupposed in speech.

Truth seems to be the cornerstone of the society in general and the communicative practice in particular. Mendacity, lying, and deception are condemned on the grounds of both morality and the potential success of communicative interaction. A member of the society, or a communicator who wants to operate smoothly, must be truthful.

WHEREVER YOU LOOK . . .

It seems, however, that everyday experience tells us that we are far from being universally and constantly truthful. We lie not to offend others; we lie to get away with being late for work or not meeting a deadline. The intuition that deception is something normal rather than abnormal in our lives and communicative practices is confirmed by numerous studies (e.g., Barnes, 1994; Nyberg, 1993; Zagorin, 1990). Robinson (1996) adds that the attitude of a truth addict seems to be doomed and that the ideal of truth becomes not more than a recipe for exploitation for those who subscribe to it. Lies and, more generally, deception are everywhere, in both the public and private spheres of our lives—in everyday life (e.g., Chovil, 1994; Cody & McLaughlin, 1990; O'Hair & Cody, 1994; Stebbins, 1975), in politics (e.g., Gruber, 1993; Hall-Jamieson, 1992; Robinson, 1993, 1994, 1996), and in the mass media (e.g., Bell, 1991; Geis, 1982; Weaver, 1994). They affect not only bureaucracies (e.g., Martin, 1982; Wilson, 1991), the military (e.g., Daniel & Herbig, 1982b; Howard, 1992; Sexton, 1986), advertising (e.g., Burke, DeSarbo, Oliver, & Robertson, 1988; Preston, 1994; Richards, 1990; Tanaka, 1994), commerce (e.g., Peters, 1987; Reece & Ducoffe, 1987), and business (e.g., Englehardt & Evans, 1994; O'Hair & Friedrich, 1992) but also the courts and police (e.g., Epstein, 1982; Kassin, Williams, & Saunders, 1990; Shuy, 1993, 1998). Neither sports (Mawby & Mitchell, 1986), literature (e.g., Adams, 1990; Kazimierski, 1996), or even the academe itself (e.g., Broad & Wade, 1982; Nawrocka, 1996) is exempt.

In the next two sections, I shall briefly deal with the ubiquity of deception in our lives. In the case of public life, I shall take on board politics and governmental bureaucracy—both claiming to act in our, the citizens', interest. I shall finish this part of the discussion by a brief reference to problems of advertising and organizational communication. Then I shall go on to discuss those aspects of interpersonal communication that are particularly prone to result in deception.

Public Domain: Politics and Bureaucracy

All those who have visited or spent some time in the United Kingdom within the last several years and either watched television or, better still, read newspapers are unlikely not to have encountered some news concerning deception in public life: a few scandals about allegations of ministers lying to the parliament, multiple allegations of politicians' wrongdoing (e.g., the cash-for-questions affair that had its turbulent turn in the days leading to the 1997 general election and that still occasionally draws the media's attention), the so-called Nolan committee formed to investigate the allegations of sleaze and make recommendations to improve the standards of the political sphere—the list could go on, and the British public has already had some opportunity to witness similar allegations but concerning the new Labour administration. Indeed, the former Welsh secretary, Ron Davies, whose resignation was shrouded in a cloud of secrecy and suspicions of deception, is another good case in point. At times, it seemed that the British political elite did hardly anything else but either accuse each other of or deny deception.

Of course, allegations (sometimes proved, sometimes not) of deception are not a British speciality. Bailey (1988), for example, shows lies in the political process in the Soviet Union, China, and the United States. Among those most famous are probably President Nixon's denials of the knowledge of Watergate and President Johnson's invention of his military record (Robinson, 1996). Finally, after the turbulence of presidential elections, recent history of Poland saw the resignation of a prime minister over allegations of espionage activities and a whole series of accusations of mendacity from the ex-premier toward the minister accusing him and vice versa. The decision of who lied is unlikely to be reached even in the courts.

Public perceptions of the political sphere are hardly any better. Addressing the problem of public trust in political communication, Robinson (1996) concludes that those on the receiving end of the political message, whether mediated or not, have little or no trust at all in what they hear or read. None of British students surveyed by Robinson believed that governments—politicians of all persuasions—did not lie at all. Politicians share this hardly honorable position only with advertisers and the tabloid the *Sun*! Moreover, although political lying always meets with condemnation of at least 50% of respondents in the British national sample, only the situation of ministers lying about health hazards ranks within the first four of most strongly condemned actions (with 68% of respondents judging it as seriously wrong and 28% as wrong; p. 257). The most strongly condemned situations did not concern the realm of politics: Financiers defrauding older persons of their savings (88% and 11%, respectively), people posing as collectors for money for charities (76% and 27%), and police forging evidence to get "guilty" verdicts (78% and 18%) were the first three most condemned situations. Given today's political junctures, it seems that only ministers talking about British beef and its safety for human consumption should really be on their guard to get their versions of the story right. As for the rest, the public at large seems to condemn them with simply not caring all that much. The truth demand on political discourse seems to be weaker and weaker.

The scale of the problem is shown by Weaver (1994). The data he quotes show a dramatic decrease in people's confidence in the political system during the last several decades. In 1958, only 24% of U.S. respondents thought that quite a lot of those running the government were a little crooked; in 1990, however, 50% thought so. Even more startling is that in 1990, only 9% of respondents thought that hardly any of those in government were crooked, with the equivalent figure for 1958 being 26% (Weaver, 1994, p. 19). The same falloff can be observed in the public's confidence in both legislative and executive authorities of the United States. Although in 1973, 24% of respondents had a great deal of confidence in the U.S. Congress, in 1993 only 7% admitted to it. The percentage of those with hardly any confidence, on the other hand, rose from 15% in 1973 to 41% in 1993 (p. 20). But then Bourdieu (1991) suggests that political propositions or programs are never logically verifiable. They are true only insofar as the person who is making them is able or, indeed, willing to translate them into action.

The other sphere of public life with which the so-called ordinary person has contact on an everyday basis is bureaucracy, the set of events and processes happening in the institutions of state (cf. Sarangi & Slembrouck, 1996). It seems that within its realm, the operation of the assumption of truthfulness ceases. Sarangi and Slembrouck point out that the assumption that applicants or clients will tell the truth not only is subject to scrutiny but also is tested by various declarations. It is only the cooperative behavior of the institutions that seems to be beyond any doubt. The recent surge of citizens' charters in the United Kingdom, however, may presuppose that reality is not as rosy as some institutions might want it.

Organizations assume implicitly that we may lie. The declaration of truthfulness on an application form is only a beginning of the distrust that public and private organizations show toward their clients. It is far from enough to tell the Department of Social Security in the United Kingdom that one is entitled to receive child benefit, for example. The applicant is required to prove that a child has actually been born. Moreover, the new 1997 immigration regulations require British employers to make sure that whoever they employ is actually allowed to work in Britain. British universities must ensure that their students are entitled to study. In practice, foreigners have to prove that they have the right to work or study. In more mundane practice, this borders on institutional racism because there are groups of citizens who are more likely than others to be asked for the proof.

Private enterprises follow suit. Again, it is not enough to tell one's motor insurance company that one has however many years of no-claims bonus; one actually has to send the certificate to the company. On the other hand, the amount of the discount one is entitled to with a no-claims bonus is hardly subjected to the scrutiny of the client.

Universities and publishers require authors of texts to be assessed or published to sign a declaration that the work they are submitting is theirs and theirs only. The requirement to prove that I do not deceive occurs almost everywhere I turn. Even my checks with which I have paid my hairstylist (yes!) for the last 6 years always have to be supported by a check guarantee card. I know he trusts me, but . . .

But then Robinson (1996) shows that it is not only politicians, the media, and other organizations that lie to us. We also lie to them. British Telecom is quoted to say that it received 100 false calls a day after an explosion at London's Victoria station. Home and overseas insurers say that they pay £50 million in bogus claims. Phony claims for unemployment and other benefits and, most of all, false tax returns—phenomena clearly not particular to any one country or even region of the world—amount to astronomical figures—the bill that in one way or another will have to be footed by the taxpayer. It seems that the precautions taken by organizations are not entirely a figment of suspicious imagination.

The final and probably one of the most obvious spheres of public communication potentially related to deception is that of advertising. Although Barnes (1994) describes advertising as ambiguous with regard to deception, an already quoted survey of British students carried out by Robinson (1996) shows that advertisers are judged the second most likely to lie, second only to the *Sun*. None of the students surveyed believed that advertisers never lied, and as many as 83% of the students thought that the advertisers lied often (p. 256).

This concern seems to be shared by the authorities, who are placing more and more constraints on advertising and the claims they make (e.g., Preston, 1994; also Richards, 1990). Preston lists as many as 14 types of implications deceptively used by advertisers and banned by the law.

Yet having bought a carton of fruit juice today that carried a notice that the juice contained "no color or preservative according to legislation," I am no longer sure whether the legislation goes far enough, let alone whether the juice my family and I have drunk does or does not have colors or preservatives.

Deceiving Thy Neighbor

Not only do we deceive the government or organizations, but also we are prepared to deceive each other. Turner, Edgley, and Olmstead (1975) report a study of 130 respondents' conversations, in which as many as 61.5% of utterances were identified to have included some form of deception (p. 72). Hample (quoted in Robinson, 1996, p. 89) estimated a rate of 13.03 lies per week per person. Although we probably tell the truth more often than not, deception is firmly established in our everyday communication. Evasion, secrecy, and even lying can be functional in interpersonal relationships. In a study carried out by Metts (1989), 357 university students reported what they saw as a situation involving deception in a close relationship. Deception, whether by commission (saying something that misses the truth) or omission (withholding information), had an important role in attempts to avoid hurting the partner, maintain face or self-image, or avoid an unpleasant scene or others (see also Miller, Mongeau, & Sleight, 1986).

Also, formal interpersonal interactions are not free from deception. Salespeople almost immediately come to mind when it comes to everyday deception. The dislike of them—or is it distrust?—is great enough for one of U.K.'s insurance companies to advertise itself by promising its potential clients that no salesperson would call. Just phone free of charge, and you won't be bothered, but perhaps also, you won't be conned. In his monograph on influencing people, Cialdini (1985) confesses to have found employment as a car salesman to gain hands-on experience in the trade tricks of getting people to buy things that they do not really want to buy or, better still, that they have no idea about what they actually are buying. Incidentally, with all the experience, he still describes his own failure to defend himself against a lowball technique.

We deceive even in encounters apparently demanding total honesty. According to Burgoon, Callister, and Hunsaker (1994), we are never totally honest even with our doctors. It is possible and, indeed, easy to sympathize with patients (while deploring the system!) who lie about their symptoms, fearing the *actual* ones would provoke treatment not covered by their insurance or further expensive testing. Patients' lying to get the doctor to continue certain medication, concealing symptoms in the hope that they would go away, and understating certain symptoms for fear of the diagnosis, however, are, at the very least, puzzling. Burgoon at al. (1994) posit that although falsification is frequently used by less than 10% of patients, it occurs with frequency sufficient enough to cause at least concern (p. 18). The drive to deceive, for whatever benefit, seems encroaching on the realm of our own well-being. Note also that neither pregnant women, nor, say, patients treated for high cholesterol, nor, finally, infants' parents are allowed to self-report their or their children's weight. It is always taken either by or in the presence of a nurse. I doubt that the assumption that the clients do not have or cannot operate scales entirely explains the system.

Deception is a means of constructing and maintaining a preferable version of reality (cf. Robinson, 1996). Regardless of whether it is detrimental or beneficial to its addressee, or its victim, deception always seems to be aimed at gaining an advantage for the speaker (e.g., Goffman, 1969). The advantage of benign fabrications, as Goffman (1986; see also Lippard, 1988) calls them, can be outsmarting the interlocutor (for example, by kidding or performing a practical joke, especially on April Fools' Day—the institutionalized 24 hours of allowed deception). It can be getting the child to do something that the parent believes to be right, or correct, and also to save the other's face after a disastrous party without running the risk of losing one's own. Exploitative actions (Goffman, 1986) take the other pole of the spectrum. Here we shall find actions aimed at getting away with something, presenting oneself in a false light, or intimidating the other.

These two poles of the spectrum—benign as against exploitative deceptions—can be assessed with regard to social sanction: The former are likely to be acceptable, the latter are not. There are, however, numerous actions that fall somewhere in between the categories. Goffman's (1990) account of information control in cases relating to social stigmas is a case in point. The concealment or manipulation of a stigma (hiding a scar behind large dark glasses, for example) often takes the form of deception, yet it is difficult to classify it as either benign or exploitative. The need to preserve face, or to project a certain self-concept, may outweigh the desire to condemn deception. The same would probably apply to a lot of the cases of patient deception referred to above. However they are classified, the deceiver's actions are still aimed at gaining a tactical advantage of a sort.

Not only do we lie at times, but also we think that we are lied to. British students, again, think that there is not one group of people that would not lie at least occasionally, including scholars, the clergy, family, good friends, and even the best friend (Robinson, 1996). The truth bias does not hold firmly when it comes to language users' actions—we all lie—and neither does it feature prominently in our beliefs about ourselves. The need to be polite, be attractive, or, finally, get someone to do something (cf. Lippard, 1988) is greater than the need to speak the truth. Deception is more often than not an easy option for dealing with a situation of avoidance—avoidance conflict (Bavelas, Black, Chovil, & Mullett, 1990a), in which all the "straight" messages available to the speaker lead in one way or another to a conclusion that is perceived negatively by the speaker. As Bavelas, Black, Chovil, and Mullett (1990b) argue, equivocation and, by extension, deception offer a way out, a possible regaining of control of the interaction.

The Sacred Tradition?

At Christmas, my parents used to leave a window open in our home so that the Starman (Polish *Gwiazdor*) could slip in and leave his gifts for me under the tree. Just as I used to, probably millions of children believe that Santa Claus, Father Christmas, the Starman, the Angel, or the Infant brings their gifts at Christmas. We, their parents, knowing quite well that this is not the case, are quite happy to continue telling our offspring that we had nothing to do with the presents they find under the trees on Christmas Eve or Christmas Day. To avoid a detailed account of human physiology, parents in Poland are also quite happy to tell their children that children are not really born but are brought by a stork or, alternatively, found in cabbage fields. Our traditions, our cultural practices, seem to abound in instances of deception. Deception is also what we are taught about in history classes. Starting with Odysseus and his Trojan horse and ending with, say, the *Fortitude South* plan seeking to persuade Nazi forces that the Allied landing in Europe in 1944 would happen in the Pas de Calais region, our history is full of acts of deception and, depending on whether they are *ours* or *theirs,* we are more or less likely to accept them. After all, we are uniquely great in our ways through history (cf. Billig, 1995).

Probably no society is without some culturally inherited practices that are deceptive, with their deceptiveness both widely known and not. Cultures are full of practices that are sanctioned although they are deceptive and practices whose deceptiveness is known only to those performing them, such as, for example, claiming that some naturally occurring phenomena or phenomena engendered by a human being are a result of gods' wrath. Zagorin (1990) proposes that deception in its dissimulating form (i.e., concealing and being secretive) played a major role in the religious and intellectual life of Western Europe both in the Middle Ages and in the 16th and 17th centuries. Such deceptive practices as "miracle management" or the sale of saints' relics have been shown to play a strategic role in the activities of the medieval Church and especially in increasing the vulnerability of the faithful (see Guriewicz, 1987; Tuchman, 1993; also Delumeau, 1983/1994).

Studies by Anderson (1986), Basso (1987), Gilsenan (1976), Perry (n.d.), and Roberts and Nutini (1988) show cultural practices being ridden by deception. Whether research is on tricksters among the Kalapalo (Basso, 1987), bloodsucking witches among the Tlaxcalans (Roberts & Nutini, 1988), or con-artistry or impersonation among the Saami (Anderson, 1986), these studies and numerous others show how universal deception is in cultures of the world. Going even further, Gilsenan (1976) shows not only that lying is necessary for the preservation of a particular way of life of a society but also that it makes life possible.

Polish traditional culture shows a number of sanctioned deceptive practices; some are a result of a belief or a practice whose upholding is more crucial than committing an act of deception. Thus Zadrozynska (1988) discusses a practice of showing evidence of the bride's virginity. Sheets stained with blood, of various origins including animals' blood, were always shown to the expectant family and guests after the "first" night. On the other hand, Stomma (1986) shows that the entirety of the moral code (with deception condemned) was suspended when one was dealing with strangers. Thus, although one would not lie to one's neighbor, lying to a stranger was a reason for glory.

Finally, if Polish national identity was, at least in part, formed by the literature of the 19th century, and more particularly by Sienkiewicz's trilogy on Polish 17th-century wars (see Kloskowska, 1996), then in part it was formed by a notorious liar. Zagloba, a knight with the type of honor that allowed him to plot his—now proverbial in Poland—*fortele* (schemes, tricks, or deceptions) or lie through his teeth, was one of the best loved characters in the novels (note the similar status of Baron Münchhausen in German-speaking countries). Similarly, just about every Pole read a dramatized account of the battle of Grunwald (German Tannenberg) in 1415 in *Krzyzacy* ("Teuton Knights"), also by Sienkiewicz. (Those who did not are more than likely to have watched the film adaptation shown on Polish television at regular intervals.) The battle, one of the most important in Polish history, as well as one constitutive of Polish identity (Kloskowska, 1996), was won by King Wladyslaw Jagiello by an act of deception—or, perhaps, as it is passed on in the Polish tradition, by an act of a wise and cunning man who did what every Pole would and should have done, too.

Indeed, the military tradition all the way until the present is particularly abundant in stories of deception. Plans Barbarossa (German campaign to mislead Stalin and achieve a surprise attack in June 1942) and Barclay (deception plan for the invasion of Sicily in 1943; cf. Daniel & Herbig, 1982a) are now classical examples of military deception. Surprise attacks (take, for example, the attack on Iraq in the Gulf War) are normally good as long as we do them and not the enemy (take Japan's attack on Pearl Harbor!). Great military deceivers remain great military commanders as long as they are our own, and as such, we shall praise them for their achievements.

The sanctioning of military deception (on our side) in reality has been translated into the practice of popular culture. Such positive characters as James Bond or Dirty Harry have no particular problems with deception. Both they and we know that it is all in the good cause and, biting our fingernails, we support them in their cause. Also, such impeccable characters as Captain Jean-Luc Picard, let alone Captain James T. Kirk, both from *Star Trek,* occasionally break the rules (do they, indeed?) and cheat the Romulans, Klingons, or some other aliens. One of the building blocks of the Kirk character is that he cheated on one of his tests. He reprogrammed the parameters of a war game that otherwise was impossible to win. And don't we like him for that! The only two characters who never lie on Starship *Enterprise* are Mr. Spock, an alien from the planet Vulcan, whose people are incapable of lying, and Lieutenant Commander Data, an android! No human being could be trusted?

ATTITUDES

Although deception seems to be a frequent, universal, and, to a considerable extent, culturally acceptable behavior, people do not approve of it and find it morally reprehensible (see Bok, 1978). Lying, Bok adds, requires a reason; truthfulness does not. Although those lies with tragic or unjust overtones are condemned the most strongly, those without such consequences are still judged negatively on the basis that "a lie is a lie" (see Robinson, 1996, p. 267). The truth bias not only is sanctioned culturally but also shows itself explicitly in people's attitudes. The results of a Gallup poll discussed by Robinson (1996; see also Robinson, 1994) show that no deceptive action taken in public life meets with condoning. Only advertisers greatly exaggerating what washing products can do were given relative sanction to do so—only 46% of persons ($N = 994$) deemed it either wrong or seriously wrong. The rest of deceptive actions in the public domain attracted condemnation of a majority of people, with newspapers' publication of untrue stories about the sexual life of famous people being the second weakest condemned action, with 68% of people judging it as either wrong or seriously wrong. Robinson (1994, 1996) also argues that the moral condemnation of deception is unlikely to be influenced by the contrast between public and interpersonal communication. Furthermore, in a study of perceptions of expectation violations, Millar and Tesser (1988) report that participants experienced a feeling of guilt because of their deceptive actions. Deception was viewed as a breach of the "proper" conduct.

One could say that it is not all that surprising, that intuitively we all know that we should not lie, and that liars are not exactly the type of people we want to deal with. The problem, however, is that as Robinson (1996) reports, we are not prepared to do anything about lies or people who lie. The feeling of disgust we feel is rarely translated into action. Robinson's look at "a year in Britain" shows persuasively just that: The cash-for-questions affair and the Pergau Dam scandal are examples of how two events potentially revealing the mendacity of the British establishment faded away in the media with the public none the wiser as to what "really" happened. No sacking (paradoxically, apart from one newspaper editor trying to expose the Pergau Dam affair), no resignation of members of the Parliament followed. Incidentally, the cash-for-questions affair had made headlines again during the 1997 election campaign in Britain and had seemingly led to the electoral defeat of one of its main figures. The voters had their chance to say what they thought, yet legally the matter remains unresolved.

Now, although the public may think that members of organizations have a primary obligation to the well-being of the society, those who blow the whistle can enjoy no more than a distant moral support of their fellow citizens, rather than their ardent wish either to help the whistle-blower or to punish those against whom the whistle is blown (Robinson, 1996). Robinson comments further that it is the accuser, rather than the accused, who is more likely to be deserted by colleagues; it is the former who will be described as out-group and have negative attributes ascribed to his or her character. Incidentally, the recent scandal within the European Commission saw the person who blew the whistle on the seemingly widespread corruption in Brussels immediately sacked. Only the apparent scale of the problem did not allow the politicians to keep the lid on the affair and led to changes. The affair was probably one of the reasons why the British government announced plans to introduce legislation protecting those who want to blow the whistle.

Still, the truth may be the coveted ideal, and deception, on the other hand, may be the shunned reality, yet we as members of societies having those value systems are not really prepared to act on the whistle. The cultural advice we seem to be getting is to shut up—tell the truth if possible, and if not, well, as long as it does not come out . . .

THE CORNERSTONE OF HUMANITY?

It seems that it would be wrong to speak of deception as some strange, unnatural, or occasional behavior. Deception is firmly situated in our everyday actions. Although we know we should not deceive others, our cultural practices, our traditions, provide us with a multitude of situations not only in which one deceives the other but, indeed, in which such actions are decidedly positive or, at the least, are not considered negative. Historical accounts—tradition—and cultural practice, as well as everyday interactions, send an ambiguous message: Tell the truth, but, at the same time, we are told to deceive: to evade, withhold information, or tell sometimes not-so-white lies. Young Americans, Britons, Poles, and Russians, from the early days of their conscious life, will see that deception is very much part of their everyday surroundings and that it has been for a long time. The truth bias is doomed not only because of the vested interests Robinson (1996) warns us of but also because of the nature of the human condition.

Must we have deception, then? The evidence of evolution, for once, answers the question positively. Humans are not alone in their deceptive practices. From simple mimicry to elaborate deception in primates (e.g., Mitchell, 1986; also Whiten & Byrne, 1988), deception occurs on just about every level of the evolution pyramid. Aitchison (1996) goes as far as suggesting that lying may be the ultimate goal in language learning. Is deception the cornerstone of humanity, then?

Aitchison (1996) discusses deception as displacement: the ability to speak of absent or even nonexistent events. The skill of displacement is one of the prerequisites of language. Now, if lying is one of the ways in which displacement in language manifests itself, the ability to lie seems to be one of those crucial skills that humans had to evolve to master language.

Must we have deception, then? It does seem so, although scholars such as Bok (1978) argue that a society in which truthful and deceptive statements were chosen at random would be undermined at the outset. But then, what I have said above suggests that to have truth and truth only around us would simply be, if nothing else, too boring to bear. Moreover, argues Barnes (1994), Machiavellian skill is an asset that contributes to our general well-being, as long as it is used in moderation and with restraint.

Whether a necessary aspect of human nature or perhaps only a human weakness—an irritating aspect of the way we are—deception has been and is part of our lives, and it seems that it is going to stay with us, at least for the foreseeable future. Just how it can manifest itself in the way we communicate with each other using language in public is what this book is all about.

METHODOLOGY AND DATA

I shall be studying deception from a discourse analytical point of view. This means that my analyses of language as a means to deceive will go beyond the boundaries of the syntactic or semantic form of the utterance. Although aware of the lexico-grammatical resources of the language system, I shall also be interested in their functions within the utterance as well as the utterance's functions within the context in which it appears. Furthermore, discourse analysis, as van Dijk (1997) points out, not only is interested in the formal (phonological or syntactic) aspects of discourse, or language use, but also focuses on social actions accomplished by language users who communicate both within certain social situations and within society and culture.

Concentrating on those applicable to my study, I offer below a résumé of what van Dijk (1997) proposes are the currently prevailing principles of discourse analysis.

1. Discourse analysis is interested in naturally occurring text (written) and talk (verbal). "Real data" that are analyzed are not in any way edited or sanitized but are studied as they are, or close to their actual form in the contexts in which they occurred.

The data that I shall analyze come mostly from British and U.S. political debates and interviews shown on British television from 1994 to 1996. In total, my corpus comprises approximately 60 hours' worth of debates and interviews. In Chapters 5 and 6, I shall also use excerpts from two 1995 Polish presidential debates and one interview broadcast on Polish television.

2. Discourse is studied within its global and local context, preferably, as a constitutive part of the context, that is, settings, participants and their communicative and social roles, goals, relevant social knowledge, norms and values, and institutional or organizational structures.

3. Discourse is a form of social practice in its sociocultural context. Language users are not isolated individuals; rather, they are engaged in communicative activities as members of groups, institutions, or cultures.

4. The accomplishment of discourse is linear and sequential. This means that units of discourse are to be explained in relation to those that precede them. It may also mean that later elements may have particular functions with respect to previous ones (for example, answers following questions).

5. Constitutive units of discourse may also be constructive of larger units, creating in such a way hierarchical structures. Language users, moreover, are capable of using those units functionally in constructing or understanding the hierarchy of discourse.

6. Discourse analysis is interested in levels or layers of discourse, attempting, however, to mutually relate one to another. The levels represent different types, on the one hand, different construction units (sounds, words, and syntactic

forms), and, on the other hand, different dimensions of discourse operation (linguistic actions and forms of interaction).

7. Language users and analysts are interested in meaning. Two types of questions are possible to ask in relation to meaning—not only the question of "What does she or he mean in this situation?" (see also Leech, 1983) but also, "Why is this being said or meant in this situation?"

8. Language, discourse, and communication in general are rule governed. On the one hand, they may be the (strict, "all-or-nothing") grammatical rules, but on the other hand, they may be the ("softer" and negotiable) principles of interaction (see also Thomas, 1995). The study of actual discourse, furthermore, focuses not only on how certain rules or principles are followed but also on how they are violated, ignored, or suspended (see also, e.g., Brown & Levinson, 1987; Grice, 1975).

Indeed, this study is devoted in its entirety to examining communicative actions whose essence is the violation of the presumption that speakers will normally tell the truth, nothing but the truth . . . It is a study of uncooperative communicative actions in the sense that the speakers/deceivers violate their addressees'/targets' expectations as to what type of communicative interaction they will be engaging in.

9. Finally, this study is designed to study strategic discourse. It assumes that language users can use their communicative actions not only to achieve understanding but also to achieve local or global communicative, social, or political goals, some of which may also be concealed from the addressee. In this book, I am interested in actions that are necessarily clandestine. Deceivers who are found out are unlikely to achieve their goal of duping the addressees.

Having espoused the above assumptions of discourse analysis, the book is methodologically eclectic. My study draws primarily on two main domains. The first, and more important in this study, is what Blum-Kulka (1997) described as discourse pragmatics with its two main areas: speech act theory and Gricean pragmatics. Although the former is interested in how communicative intentions are conventionally encoded in the linguistic text, the latter is more concerned with the ways in which communicators recognize (or fail to recognize) their intentions in what is communicated (cf. Blum-Kulka, 1997). Toward the end of the book, the theory of politeness (Brown & Levinson, 1987) will also provide a relevant theoretical basis.

The second domain, with which, again, I have predominantly engaged toward the end of the book, is the tenets and assumptions of critically oriented linguistics and discourse analysis (e.g., Hodge & Kress, 1993), drawing heavily on functional linguistics, most particularly that of Halliday (e.g., 1994). I shall use this perspective particularly in Chapter 7 in the analysis of discursive representations of agency in evasive responses. Rather than presenting these perspectives in detail here, however, I hope to do it more usefully at those stages of my discussion when they will be drawn on directly.

2

What Is Deception?

Research into deception has been one of the major areas of investigation within the study of communication for the last two or three decades, particularly in the United States. Communication scientists have researched deception mainly along two major avenues (cf. Miller, deTurck, & Kalbfleisch, 1983; also Miller & Stiff, 1993): people's ability to detect deceptive messages (e.g., Burgoon, Buller, Ebesu, White, & Rockwell, 1996; Ekman, 1985; Stiff & Miller, 1986; also Kalbfleisch, 1994) and verbal as well as nonverbal correlates of deception (e.g., DePaulo, 1988; Ekman, 1988; O'Hair, Cody, & McLaughlin, 1981). The emphasis on detection and leakage of deception resulted in the paucity of texts with theoretical or programmatic objectives. The shortage is even more acute when it comes to studies that take the message and its design as the point of departure (cf. McCornack, 1992). The recent claim made by Buller and Burgoon (1994) that such criticisms did not apply any longer is still overoptimistic (cf. McCornack, 1997). Indeed, the latest books that deal with deception either discuss it within a broader perspective and thus do not explore it in any detail (see Ng & Bradac, 1993; Parret, 1994; Shuy, 1998), view the matter from sociological or sociocultural perspectives (see Bailey, 1991; Barnes, 1994), or, finally, approach deception from the vantage point of (social) psychology (cf. Bavelas, Chovil, & Mullett, 1990a; Miller & Stiff, 1993; Robinson, 1996). Furthermore, with the exception of the books by Ng and Bradac (1993) and Bavelas and her associates (1990a), all of them—as is usually true of deception research in general—are by and large interested only in lying, leaving most of the vast and varied area of deceptive communication unexplored. Finally, such exceptions as the information manipulation theory proposed by McCornack (1992), although anchored within Gricean pragmatics, do not start with a general insight into the concept of deception, being content with the too general notion of violation of conversational maxims (Grice, 1975).

Aim and Scope

My objective in this chapter is twofold. First, I shall critically discuss the few attempts at conceptualizing deception that have been made and try to show that the approaches they offer are, in view of the evidence, problematic. I shall argue that defining deception as truth and falsity of the propositional content of deceptive utterances or falsity of the belief they are intended to elicit is implausible. I shall also offer what seems to me a plausible definition of deception as information manipulation.

Second, I shall critically review typologies of deceptive communicative activities. The review will be based on the following two distinctions. I shall first distinguish between deception by omission and commission. Deception by commission will be broken down further into those utterances that are attempts to deceive through explicit information and those that do it implicitly. Although the review is intended to be critical, my own approach to the problem of deceptive communication will be discussed in Chapter 3. Finally, I shall briefly indicate what might count as an overall theoretical framework within which to view deceptive communication.

THE PROBLEM OF DEFINITION

There is probably only one characteristic of deceptive communication that is widely agreed on in the literature, namely, that an act of deception has to be intended by the deceiver. Messages that are unintentionally misleading are usually described as mistakes, gaffes, and the like (e.g., Buller & Burgoon, 1994). The assumption of intentionality of deception is not made only in the applied deception research, such as deceptive advertising or military studies (see Moose, 1982; Preston, 1994; Richards, 1990). This study is underpinned by the assumption that deception is intentional.

Deception Versus Lying

Lying is normally defined as an intentionally misleading statement (cf., e.g., Coleman & Kay, 1981; Robinson, 1996; Vincent & Castelfranchi, 1981). As one of the likely prototypes of deception, the act of lying has often been used as a means of conceptualizing deceptive communication both implicitly (e.g., Zuckerman, DePaulo, & Rosenthal, 1981) and explicitly (cf. Ekman, 1985; also Bolinger, 1973). For example, Zuckerman and associates define deception as an act that is intended to foster in another person a belief or understanding that the deceiver considers false; they go on to describe it further with the two following characteristics: (a) the deceiver transmitting a false message (while hiding true information) and (b) the act being intentional.

Such a definition is implausible. There are many utterances that may be used deceptively and to which the criterion of truth or falsity does not apply. The notorious "Have you stopped beating your wife?" although neither true nor false, can clearly be deceptive. But perhaps the notion of *false message* does encompass a message with a false presupposition (an assumption carried by the utterance) or implicature (an inference triggered by the flouting of a conversational maxim; cf. Grice, 1975). Then passive deception (Handel, 1982), or deception by omission or secrecy (cf. Bok, 1982; Bradac, Friedman, & Giles, 1986; Chisholm & Feehan, 1977), consists of the deceiver's saying nothing at all and thus allowing the target to acquire a false belief or to continue having it. The problem of a false message does not even arise, simply because the message is silence (cf. Jaworski, 1993; Pisarkowa, 1986). Silence, or more generally, an incomplete utterance (i.e., one from which a piece of relevant information is withheld), can easily be deceptive, and yet it can even be truthful (cf. also Hopper & Bell, 1984; Knapp & Comadena, 1979; Watzlawick, 1976). Setting the falseness of the message as a precondition of deceptive communication does not seem to encompass the breadth of deceptive communication; neither, it seems, does the mere incorporation of omission in the definition.

Describing deception as either falseness or omission (cf. Metts, 1989; Miller, 1983) is not sufficient. It seems that an utterance both complete and truthful can still be deceptive. A speaker who knows that he or she has a reputation of a liar and knows, moreover, that the target does not believe him or her may well use such a message with a deceptive intent (a scenario discussed in Chisholm & Feehan, 1977, and Bradac et al., 1986).

Deception and False Beliefs

The way forward seems to be to define deceptive communication as false beliefs intended to be induced in the target. Indeed, with few exceptions (cf. McCornack, 1992), such an approach is prevalent in the literature. The core of such otherwise differing definitions is that deceptive communication occurs when a speaker transmits a message that is intended to create or foster a false belief in the target (e.g., Buller & Burgoon, 1994, 1996b; Ekman, 1985; Lewicki, 1983; Vincent & Castelfranchi, 1981).

Now, first, one could argue that a situation in which the speaker makes the addressee believe the proposition of the type "there are extraterrestrial civilizations" is not covered by the amended definition. Statements of this type are unverifiable, and no truth value can be ascribed to them; although they can be used to deceive, they are hardly misrepresentations (cf. Fraser, 1994). Furthermore, if it is plausible to argue that a distrusted liar can use this situation to make someone believe something false, it seems that the reverse situation could also be invoked. A liar may well say something false with the hope that the target will

infer the opposite: the truth. Such a communicative exchange is as much deceptive, because the target's beliefs as to what is true or not are misled, and it is precisely the beliefs of the parties engaged in deception that are at stake (the point
made particularly clear by Bradac et al., 1986; cf. also Bradac, 1983; Miller,
1983). In other words, the target of the deceptive act is manipulated into thinking
what suits the deceiver; that this happens to be the truth is, in my opinion, of
minor importance.[1]

    In sum, deception does in one way or another involve falsity, or perhaps
nontruth of a belief by the target—the realm of truth and falsity seems to be the
defining characteristic of deception. It may, however, be a preexisting belief on
which the success of the act of deception may be dependent. Still, the definition
of deception as inducing or reinforcing false beliefs—although perhaps encom-
passing a majority of acts of deception—does not cover all of them, and thus a
new path must be sought.

Deception as Manipulation

    A number of definitions of deception do not use the concept of truth or falsity.
Ng and Bradac (1993) propose that deceptive communicators fail to provide
message recipients with an *accurate* picture of their beliefs, or more actively,
they provide them with an inaccurate picture. There are, however, a number of
speech acts in which the speaker does not show an accurate picture of her or his
beliefs, and yet they would not normally be counted as deception. Acts of boasting, insinuations, mockery, and propaganda all imply concealing the speaker's
intentions as well as her or his beliefs regarding the utterance (e.g., Bell, 1997;
Fraser, 1994; Galasiński, 1992), and thus one could argue that the speaker does
not reveal the full picture of her or his beliefs. The Ng and Bradac definition
seems to be too broad. The same applies to the definition proposed by
McCornack (1992). He suggests viewing deception as covert violations of
Gricean (Grice, 1975) maxims of conversation. But communicative acts involving fallacies can also be defined as maxim violations (see Walton, 1995) and yet
do not have to be deceptive.

    I do not think that one needs to discard the argument proposed in these two
approaches, however. Needed is a narrowing of the scope of the definitions, for
example, a distinction between acts of violation of maxims of conversation in
general and those that pertain to the class of deception. It seems that such an
operation can be usefully made with the notion of manipulation.

    The approach I shall argue for below sees deception as a communicative act
that is intended to induce in the addressee a particular belief, by manipulating the
truth and falsity of information. The last element of the definition is aimed spe-

cifically at distinguishing between, say, deception and persuasion, two forms of manipulation that refer to two realities—the world of truth and fact and the world of value, or cultural evaluations, respectively (cf. Watzlawick, 1976).

Deception is a type of manipulation. I borrow the notion of manipulation from Puzynina (1992), who defines it as an attempt to affect the target in such a way that her or his behavior/action is an instrument of attaining the goals of the manipulator, who acts without using force but in such a way that the target does not know the goal of the manipulator's action (cf. also Bursten, 1973; Goodin, 1980; Rudinow, 1978). Deceptive communication is therefore a type of linguistic manipulation, that is, manipulation by means of texts of natural language (Puzynina, 1992) operating in the area of the truth and falsity of propositions. This definition, although clearly establishing deception within a group of related phenomena, also acknowledges that deception must in one way or another involve nontruth, not necessarily, however, an untrue message or induction of nontrue beliefs.

It is worth noting here that Miller and Stiff (1993) and, more recently, Stiff (1995) also suggest reconsideration of deception in terms of a higher-order concept. Their postulate, however, is that deception should be viewed as persuasion. Although I generally agree with the notion of viewing deception relative to a compliance-gaining strategy, I still argue that persuasion is only a subset of manipulative strategies, at the same level as deception. Although a persuader sets out to induce a belief or attitude or, indeed, action on the part the addressee, and does it also without the addressee's realizing it, this is done by setting up a system of values to which persuadees are intended to subscribe. Targets of persuasion are made to believe that something is good or bad, rather than true or false. Rather than positioning deception and persuasion as a category within each other, I submit that they both can be seen as strategies that language users employ in laying out, or imposing, a preferred version of reality. At the highest level, both persuasion and deception are attempts at discursive representation (see also Chapter 6).

Finally, some acts of manipulation are neither persuasive nor deceptive. Take the example of leading questions (cf., e.g., Dillon, 1990; Loftus, 1975; Shuy, 1993). Loftus suggests that the addressee of questions is unlikely to oppose the question's presuppositions (that which is taken for granted in the question), even if the addressee cannot commit her- or himself to their truth. In the same way, Shuy (1993) shows the mechanism of getting a child to commit to potentially untrue statements by framing the question in a way consistent with the child's worldview. In both cases, those questioned are manipulated into doing something they may not have done otherwise. In neither case is it the goal of the questioner to deceive (or indeed persuade) the targets of the claims they are making. Rather, it is to get them to testify to something without even realizing it.

THE MANY FACES OF DECEPTION

The most general distinction that is usually made within the whole class of deceptive communication is that of active and passive deception, or, as it is sometimes put, deception by omission and commission (cf., e.g., Chisholm & Feehan, 1977; Ekman, 1985; Handel, 1982). The passive deceiver does not say something that is true and relevant, inducing thereby a belief (or a set of beliefs) that does not represent the whole (relevant) picture of reality in the addressee; thus, the passive deceiver does not prevent the addressee from acquiring the belief. The active deceiver, on the other hand, says something for the addressee to acquire such a belief.

Deception by Omission

Deception by omission occurs when the speaker/deceiver withholds some information from the target. The deceiver does not issue an utterance consisting of a new proposition, although it would be true and relevant in a given situation. One who deceives by omission does not offer anything in lieu of the withheld information. A liar, for example, tells the target something she or he believes to be false and, at the same time, withholds the true information. Withholding information, controlling it, is the essence of deception in general—if the target had access to all information relevant in a given communicative situation, deception would be impossible. A passive deceiver, however, offers nothing to distort or falsify reality; the passive deceiver is silent and merely conceals a piece of information (cf., e.g., Bok, 1982; Bradac, 1983; Metts, 1989). Incidentally, the Polish language, unlike English, has a verb that refers to such situations. The Polish *przemilczec* (similar to the German *verschweigen*), which does not have to refer to a situation of deception, refers to a speaker who fails to mention something or, literally, is silent about something (for further discussion, see Jaworski, 1993).

Deception by Commission

An active deceiver, one who engages in an act of deception by commission, causally contributes to the target's acquiring or continuing a belief that suits the purposes of the deceiver. This can be done in two ways: by information explicitly conveyed in the utterance or by information that is implicit.

Deception Through Explicit Information

The lie is the prototypical act of deception, which is presumably why it has attracted most attention in deception research. Typically, lies are defined as those messages that consist of a false statement (while the speaker knows it is false) intended to mislead the addressee (cf., e.g., Coleman & Kay, 1981; Hopper & Bell, 1984; Robinson, 1996). The problem with such definitions, however, is the tacit assumption that lies are "objectively" false. Bradac et al. (1986) argue, however, that it is a particular set of a speaker's beliefs that constitutes a lie, rather than a relationship between the utterance and the extralinguistic state of affairs. The condition of the speaker's believing that her or his utterance is false is sufficient for the utterance to count as a lie. Also, the opposite is the case: A speaker cannot be held accountable for lying if the speaker says something that he or she believes is the case, although "objectively," it is not. Otherwise, all those who said that there were only eight planets in our solar system would have had to be called liars in 1929 just because Pluto had not yet been discovered (an example given in Fraser, 1994).

Lies, therefore, are statements (they have to be utterances to which the criterion of truth or falsity is applicable) that the speaker believes to be false and that are intended to mislead the addressee (cf. Bok, 1978). The latter condition (intention to mislead) is necessary to exclude communicative acts that are false but not intentionally misleading, or that are even intended to be recognized as false. Such communicative acts as irony, jokes, and teasing are neither types of lying nor, indeed, deception, as Hopper and Bell (1984; see also Buller & Burgoon, 1994) propose. First, such acts are not intended to mislead, and, second, the truth of the propositions in the utterances is irrelevant—they are not meant to be either true or false; their assessment in those terms is suspended (cf. Sweetser, 1987). On the other hand, white lies, social lies, or fibs (cf., e.g., Sweetser, 1987; Robinson, 1996) are still lies. The differences between them and "lies proper" are only social. They all convey false information intended to mislead, but at the same time, they all are, to some extent at least, justified by rules of politeness or the harmlessness of the message. Their nature within the perspective of deception is, however, unchanged—they all are false statements intended to mislead (cf. Verschueren, 1985).

Half-truths or distortions are usually discussed as the other part of active deception, complementary to false utterances (cf., e.g., Buller & Burgoon, 1994; Ekman, 1985; Garfinkel, 1977; Metts, 1989; Turner et al., 1975). In different studies, however, the area allotted to these types of utterances is demarcated differently. For example, they are shown as consisting of such categories as exaggeration, minimization, or equivocation (e.g., Metts, 1989). Alternatively, separate categories are created to cover more or less the same types of acts of communication. Thus, Turner and associates (1975) prefer to distinguish between exaggerations and half-truths, whereas Buller and Burgoon (1994) propose to differentiate between the categories of exaggerations/fictions and half-truths. Finally, Burgoon, Buller, Guerrero, Afifi, and Feldman (1996) based their research on three types of deception: falsification, concealment, and equivocation.

Although the different studies seem to refer to the same types of utterances, the conceptualizations they offer differ significantly. For Turner and associates (1975), exaggerations are overstatements giving more information than required; half-truths, on the other hand, deceive by providing less information. Yet Metts (1989) takes both categories (calling them exaggerations and minimizations, respectively), adds equivocation, and calls the group *distortions,* defining it as manipulation with truth. Although the categories of exaggeration and minimization in Metts's typology may be uncontroversial, it is unclear why they are grouped together with equivocation. Metts is content with simply proposing that the midpoint of the three-point deception continuum, from overt to covert misrepresentation, is occupied by a cluster of messages that distort reality in different degrees: by evading, exaggerating, or minimizing. In the ensuing discussion of the typology, however, evading disappears and equivocation is added. Metts does not offer any indication how the messages in this cluster may be related to one another, particularly how evasion or equivocation may be related to the other two, or, indeed what the distorting capacities of evasion are. In the same way, the rationale behind Turner et al.'s (1975) typology is unclear.

Buller and Burgoon (1994), in turn, define half-truths as a mix of truthful and dishonest information yet do not offer any explanation of what that may mean. Might it be that in one turn the speaker both lies and tells the truth? Or perhaps the mix is more tightly distributed within one act, for example, the speaker tells truthfully where she or he was but tells a lie about when it was? The other category, complementing half-truths, is also problematic. Exaggerations/fictions are defined as consisting of distortions, myth, make-believing, and white lies. It is unclear why distortions are put on a par with white lies, which, as I said above, are still falsifications. It is even more unclear why myths are placed in the same category. Even if one assumes a "lay" understanding of myth (as opposed to anthropological; see Eliade, 1966, or Lévi-Strauss, 1963, in which case myth is likely to be construed as understood as metaphoric or symbolic truth), then myth either is not perceived as true or is perceived as a tale whose truth is irrelevant. The typology proposed by Buller and Burgoon (1994) mixes together acts of communication distinguished by different criteria—on the one hand, the relationship of an utterance to reality relative to its truthfulness and, on the other, the social functioning of false utterances.

More generally, it seems that the main problem of the discussed typologies, and indeed, a number of others (cf., e.g., Ekman, 1985; Hopper & Bell, 1984) is that they do not seem to be based on a clear set of criteria. Despite the claims to the contrary (Buller & Burgoon, 1994), the aforementioned typologies are based largely on perceptions of deceptive messages either by participants or by coders who try to fit the elicited data into preconceived categories provided by the researcher. Indeed, Metts (1989) provides herself with an escape category that consists of messages that are too vague to be coded. The linguistic turn on which Hopper and Bell (1984) claim to have based their typology offers hardly any alternative. Although their attempt is based on linguistic labels of acts of deception, they do not attempt any semantic analysis of the corpus (of the sort carried out, for example, by Verschueren, 1985). Their typology is based on a highly heterogeneous corpus in which *evasion* is made to sit next to *back-stabbing.*

The last type of deceptive strategy that is discussed in the literature is equivocation. Metts (1989) mentions it in her discussion of the midpoint of the covert-overt spectrum; Buller and Burgoon (1994) allow for some ambiguities to be deceptive yet do not include equivocation in their typology; finally, Burgoon, Buller, Guerrero, et al. (1996) position it as one of the three types of deception (next to falsification and concealment). Although the former two studies do not attempt to define equivocation in any way, the latter does. Burgoon, Buller, Guerrero, et al. propose that equivocation is characterized by ambiguity, indirectness or irrelevance, and depersonalization.

It seems that equivocation is seen here in at least two dimensions: on the one hand, semantic—an equivocal message is vague or ambiguous. On the other hand, equivocation is also defined conversationally, as an indirect or irrelevant response. It is unclear how the two levels relate to each other, and yet an utterance that is indirect in the sense of pertaining to the group of indirect speech acts (e.g., Searle, 1975) may well be unequivocal semantically. Conventional utterances such as "Can you pass the salt, please?" are hardly vague or ambiguous, but they are indirect. There are similar problems with the definition proposed by Bavelas and associates (1990a). Defining equivocation as nonstraightforward, ambiguous, or obscure, they also propose to see indirect speech acts or evasion as equivocation.

An approach to equivocation that I advocate here has recently been proposed by Su (1994), who provides a useful distinction between ambiguity and vagueness. A linguistic item is ambiguous if, semantically, it is capable of having two or more meanings and, pragmatically, those meanings must be interpretable as tenable in a given context. Vagueness, on the other hand, introduces the presence of uncertainty of meaning; it is—as Su puts it—a "semantic nebula" (p. 116). Pragmatically, vagueness can be described as uncertainty in deciding the applicability of meaning (see also Kaluza's [1990] proposal of "uncertain meaning"). Both phenomena seem to be capable of deception, as both can render the speaker as *not* accountable for any meaning inferred (see Bradac et al., 1986). Note also a problem with regard to evasion here. Bavelas and her associates (1990a) classified it as equivocal. Whatever the sense of the word, however, it seems that evasion is a phenomenon occurring at the level of dialogue—question-answer exchange—and thus the equivocality of the utterance itself is hardly at issue. It is the relationship of the answer toward the question that is at stake, rather than the answer's clarity (see Bradac et al., 1986).

Deception Through Implied Information

Lies are the only straightforward way of deceiving people. They are utterances for which the speaker can be held accountable with regard to their falsehood. Deception, however, can also be carried out by means of nonexplicit information, one conveyed by the utterance yet not on its surface. Bowers, Elliot, and Desmond (1977) propose to call such messages devious (cf. also Bradac et al., 1986; Ng & Bradac, 1993).

With some exceptions (e.g., Bradac et al., 1986), the literature on deception either does not mention deception through implied information at all or, alternatively, sees it, more or less implicitly, as one of the types of deceptive strategy (e.g., Buller & Burgoon, 1994; Hopper & Bell, 1984; Vincent & Castelfranchi, 1981). Whether it is presupposition (e.g., Harder & Kock, 1976) or conversational implicature (Bowers et al., 1977), the messages issued with a false implication are put at the same level as other types of deceptive messages. In the next chapter, I shall argue, however, that such an approach is problematic and is a result, once again, of unclear typological criteria. The basic assumption behind my proposal is that irrespective of its explicit or implicit nature, the nature of the misleading proposition remains unchanged. The problem is only the manner in which the deceptive message is conveyed.

CONCEPTUALIZING DECEPTION

To my knowledge, there are four attempts at a comprehensive conceptualization of deception. Two of them, the information manipulation theory (IMT; McCornack, 1992) and the propositional communication approach (Bradac et al., 1986), are attempts at conceptualizing the deceptive message. The third—interpersonal deception theory (IDT)—is an attempt at an overall theory and model of interpersonal deception (see Buller & Burgoon, 1996b) within which the deceptive message itself is conceptualized. The fourth is an attempt at a general theory of deception (see Whaley, 1982). Although the first three arose on the basis of communication studies, the last one was proposed within the framework of military studies and will therefore be excluded from the discussion at this point. I shall, however, return to Whaley's theory in Chapter 5 to position linguistic deception within a general theory. The discussion below mainly reviews the theoretical approaches to the deceptive utterance. Because the conceptualization of the message within IDT (Burgoon, Buller, Guerrero, et al., 1996) is a response to that offered by IMT and is aimed at replacing it, I shall start by reviewing the latter and critique the two in view of each other. Then, I shall discuss the propositional communication proposal. Finally, I shall offer some comments as to what I see as a plausible way forward with regard to the analysis of deception in language.

Information manipulation theory (McCornack, 1992) is founded on the assumption that research into deception has ignored systematic inquiry into the deceptive message. Criticizing studies that use either the method of instructing participants to "tell a lie" or "tell the truth" or, alternatively, the recall method, McCornack goes on to argue that studying deception by coding the type of the deceptive message is also unsatisfactory (for a further critique, see also McCornack, 1997). Such procedures may result in obtaining a sample of deceptive messages that consists of the most salient examples thereof, rather than a corpus indicating how individuals deceive each other in actual conversations. Recall methods, adds McCornack (1992), are particularly useful for determining the scripts that participants have with regard to deception.

Instead, IMT proposes to look into deception as a means of manipulating information that may involve various extents to which a message contravenes the expectations of truthfulness. McCornack (1992) suggests a set of categories against which message deceptiveness can be gauged. Building on Grice's theory of cooperative principle and conversational maxims, the IMT's principal claim is that "messages that are commonly thought of as deceptive derive from covert violations of the conversational maxims" (p. 5). Indeed, Grice himself (1975) describes the violation of maxims as an unostentatious nonobservance, and a speaker who violates a conversational maxim will be liable to mislead (for a useful discussion of Grice's theory, see Thomas, 1995).

Having established the Gricean conceptual framework, McCornack (1992) shows messages that violate the four conversational maxims. Thus, omissions as well as messages involving varying degrees of informativeness violate the maxim of quantity; quality violations, being the prototypical "deceptive messages," involve "distorted" versions of the sensitive information or the presentation of completely fabricated information; speakers who violate the maxim of relation attempt to divert the course of conversation from potential disclosure of "dangerous" information; finally, manner violations involve ambiguity.

Burgoon, Buller, Guerrero, et al. (1996; cf. also Buller & Burgoon, 1996a; Jacobs, Brashers, & Dawson, 1996; Jacobs, Dawson, & Brashers, 1996; also McCornack himself [1997]), however, launch a critique of IMT and construct a different conceptual framework: interpersonal deception theory (Buller & Burgoon, 1996b; also Burgoon & Buller, 1996; see also the critique in DePaulo, Ansfield, & Bell, 1996; Stiff, 1996). IDT constructs a comprehensive model of interpersonal, face-to-face deception that is defined as a message knowingly transmitted by a sender to foster a false belief or a conclusion (Buller & Burgoon, 1996b). Deceptive messages, in turn, include three components: the central deceptive message (usually verbal), ancillary messages bolstering the verisimilitude of the deceptive message or protecting the source of deception, and, finally, inadvertent behaviors divulging the deceptive intent. The first two messages are aimed at fostering credibility; "leakage" may undermine it (p. 209).

Burgoon, Buller, Guerrero, et al. (1996) give up the Gricean framework and propose to view the deceptive message through five nonexhaustive and nonindependent fundamental dimensions: veridicality, completeness, directness/relevance, clarity, and personalization. Veridicality is the core of the conceptualization: It refers directly to Grice's maxim of quality (i.e., truthfulness) but is aimed at replacing it. Moreover, having assumed that a successful deceptive communication must appear to be truthful, the authors propose to distinguish between *actual veridicality* (the objective truth value) and *apparent veridicality* (believability of the message). The maxim of quantity (i.e., "Say as much as is necessary, not less, not more") is replaced by the category of completeness. Completeness is categorized into *informational (semantic) completeness* (the delivery of all pertinent information) and *conversational (syntactic or pragmatic) completeness* (the utterance's sufficiency in satisfying conversational demands). The maxim of relation ("Be relevant") is replaced by the notion of directness/relevance, a notion applicable to the analysis of indirect speech acts. Furthermore, a message may be *pragmatically or syntactically direct* (appearing to be a grammatically coherent sequel to the previous utterance) or *semantically direct and relevant* (providing explicit content that is related to the previous utterance).

The dimension of clarity is intended to replace the maxim of manner (roughly, "Be clear") in the Gricean approach. *Semantic clarity* refers to the comprehensibility of what is said (vague meaning); *syntactic clarity* refers to how it is said (grammatically indecipherable utterance). Finally, Burgoon, Buller, Guerrero, et al. (1996) introduce the notion of personalization, the only notion that does not stem from Grice's theory. It gauges messages with respect to whether "the information presented conveys the speaker's own thoughts, opinions, feelings" (p. 55). It is argued that deceivers employ strategies to dissociate themselves from their message. Personalization is one of the basic maxims of conversation, and self-ownership of utterances is an inherent presupposition of discourse.

Although the proposal is aimed at replacing IMT and the Gricean approach, it is difficult to see how the proposal is to achieve it. The problem is right at the level of theoretical framing. Although Burgoon, Buller, Guerrero, et al. (1996) attempt to dissociate themselves from the Gricean approach, its influence is only too obvious in the proposed model. By removing Grice's theory of cooperative principle, the IDT approach undermines its very existence, and the authors do not offer any justification for the approach they are taking. Criticizing Grice (and McCornack, 1992), as well as introducing a new maxim, pulls the conceptual construction down, while nothing is offered in its lieu.

There are, however, even more problematic aspects to this model. Let me start with what I consider its most problematic aspect: the inclusion of the "maxim" of personalization. Apart from quoting a number of studies (e.g., Bavelas et al.,

1990a) that posit that "ownership" is a matter of degree in communication and that its manipulation can be misleading, Burgoon, Buller, Guerrero, et al. (1996) do not offer any rationale for including it into what is in effect a Gricean model. The relationship between the new category and the other four is not at all clear. Note that although Bavelas and associates (1990a) list ownership of messages as one of the possible dimensions of equivocation, their model has nothing to do with the Gricean one. Finally, although an utterance such as "You are required to pay the fine now" (Burgoon, Buller, Guerrero, et al., p. 55) may indeed mask the identity of who issues the instruction, it is difficult to see why it cannot be analyzed through the Gricean maxim of quantity (the speaker withholds the piece of relevant information that it is she or he who is the originator of the instruction) or manner (the speaker is unclear). Not only can the Gricean analysis tease out the utterance's potential deceptiveness (especially when the speaker has no right to impose such a rule), but also it can render depersonalization as a masking or mitigating device (cf. Trosborg's [1997] analysis of similar devices in legal discourse). Indeed, Ng and Bradac (1993) propose that masks of this sort are not deceptive, that they do not withhold true information or propose false information; rather, they present extralinguistic reality in a partial way. Whichever is the case, depersonalization in the IDT model seems to be superfluous with regard to the Gricean approach.

There are significant problems with the model in other categories as well. Veridicality seems to be construed as the objective truth of the message, and yet it is not known how this aspect fits into the overall theory, particularly so if deceptive communication is defined as a message knowingly sent to foster a false belief rather than an "objectively" false message. On the other hand, the *apparent veridicality* is also hardly a tester for what is deceptive, as it is to be judged by receivers. In other words, veridicality, as proposed by Burgoon, Buller, Guerrero, et al. (1996), does not actually explain what counts as a deceptive message. Although criticizing IMT for its message production orientation, the researchers do not provide anything in its stead—the "objective" truth may have nothing to do with what the speaker believes to be true and thus with what information the speaker sets out to deceive the target.

The relationship is equally unclear between three other concepts, namely, (a) conversational completeness, that is, sufficiency of an utterance in satisfying current conversational demands (Burgoon, Buller, Guerrero, et al., 1996); (b) pragmatic or syntactic directness, that is, provision of a coherent sequel to the previous utterance; and (c) semantic directness or relevance, that is, providing explicit content to the previous utterance. It seems that all these concepts more or less refer to the notion of semantic and pragmatic relevance (cf. Dascal, 1977; Holdcroft, 1987). Within the categories, the differences between pragmatic and syntactic directness or semantic directness and semantic relevance are also unclear.

Finally, the distinction between semantic and syntactic clarity, in the way Burgoon, Buller, Guerrero, et al. (1996) propose it, is problematic as well. They map the distinction onto the *what* and the *how* of the message. And yet, intuitively, it seems that clarity always refers to *how* an utterance is formed. Syntactic clarity, furthermore, is described relative to producing grammatically indecipherable utterances. It is proposed that when syntactically ambiguous, "deceivers may use such devices as passive voice, indefinite referents and verb forms that make the grammatical structure unclear" (p. 54). It is again far from clear why passive voice should produce grammatically indecipherable utterances, why indefinite referents are classed as a syntactic category, and what type of verb forms the authors have in mind. The response to the McCornack, Levine, Morrison, & Lapinski's (1996) critique provided by Buller and Burgoon (1996a) does not explain the above mentioned difficulties away. What appears from this discussion is that when the IDT approach to the deceptive message is deprived of the inconsistencies referred to above, what remains is more or less the Gricean approach to deception.

The approach proposed by Bradac et al. (1986) takes the point of departure in the assumption that it is a particular constellation of beliefs that constitutes a lie or other deceptive strategies. Only the speaker her- or himself can know whether she or he lied, withheld information, or evaded an answer. The "objective" relationship between the message and the extralinguistic reality is immaterial. The speaker's beliefs can then be translated into the propositions conveyed in an utterance, and thus Bradac and associates propose a "portrait of what Speaker *plans* to do as s/he communicates propositionally with Hearer, not what is actually uttered" (p. 129). There are four axioms by which deceptive communication is viewed. First, the speaker must decide whether to produce an utterance or to remain silent; second, the speaker will intend to produce in the addressee a belief regarding her or his own belief—the former belief may be *accurate* or not. Relevance of the utterance, as believed by the speaker, is the third dimension of the analytical framework. Fourth, the speaker will have a belief as to her or his accountability for what she or he will say in the sense of having only one interpretation (Bradac et al., 1986; Ng & Bradac, 1993). On the basis of the model, Bradac et al. constructed three groups of deceptive messages: the truth-telling family (with truthful utterances, secrecy with their devious counterparts); the falsehood family (falsehood, falsehood avoidance, and their devious counterparts); and, finally, the family of evasions.

It seems that the propositional communication approach is particularly useful in highlighting that the analysis of deceptive communication should be concerned not so much with testing the relationship between the utterance and the extralinguistic reality but rather with the particular configuration of the speaker's beliefs. A liar who unknowingly happens to tell the truth is still a liar. There are a number of problems with the approach, however. The first is because Bradac et al. (1986) do not attempt to provide any rationale for the four axioms they put forward (cf. also Robinson, 1996). Moreover, it seems that the categories they propose can be likened to those within the Gricean tradition. Thus, the intention to issue an utterance seems to be an equivalent of the maxim of quantity. Both are responsible for differentiating between, roughly speaking, secrecy and deception by commission. The difference between them, however, is that the maxim of quantity seems to be more sensitive to detecting degrees of withholding information, whereas the propositional communication approach seems to propose an all-or-nothing model. Accuracy and relevance can easily be squared with the maxims of quality and relation, respectively. Accountability, referring to the message's ambiguity, clearly refers to the maxim of manner.

Although an elegant attempt at an exhaustive account of deception, the model produces unlikely messages (e.g., "devious evasion avoidance"—"the speaker withholds an irrelevant utterance while believing that s/he is not accountable for this non-utterance" (Bradac et al., 1986, p. 137), a problem acknowledged by the researchers themselves. Moreover, although the model generates four other avoidance messages, it is unclear whether the avoidance can actually be replaced by a different message. For example, although a speaker may not give an evasive answer of one type (evasion avoidance), may the speaker produce something else in its lieu, for example, another evasive answer? Bradac et al. do not account for such a possibility, nor is it clear how it would be analyzed within the model. On the other hand, the model seems incapable of handling certain types of messages. For example, partial secrecy or the potential spectrum of messages hovering between truth and falsity (cf. above and next chapter) cannot, to my mind, be accounted for within the model, precisely because of its binary approach.

Left after this critique is the Gricean approach in the form of the information manipulation theory. Before I offer my comments, let us first discuss the criticisms made by Jacobs and his associates and Buller and Burgoon (1996a). It seems that Jacobs, Dawson, and Brashers (1996; also Jacobs, Brashers, & Dawson, 1996) criticize IMT on two counts: first, for focusing on the account of deception relative to violation, arguing that conversational implicatures should be given a more prominent role in the account; and, second, on the grounds that IMT does not require the necessary violation of the maxim of quality (truthfulness) in the case of deception, which, according to the researchers, is its inherent element.

Especially the first of the charges seems problematic: In Grice's (1975) account, violations are described as unostentatious, and this is precisely why "the speaker is liable to mislead" (p. 49); an implicature, on the other hand, is an inference triggered by an ostentatious flout. Let me assume, however, that Jacobs, Dawson, and Brashers's (1996) account of the conversational implicature is plausible: An implicature does occur in an utterance that observes all the maxims and is calculated by the addressee rather than triggered by the speaker. The speaker violates the maxim of quality or quantity and thus misleads the target. But if the addressee's assumption about the speaker's cooperativeness leads to a quality violation at the level of what is implicated, this implies that deception is *negotiated* between the speaker and the addressee. Yet it seems that a violation is the speaker's deliberate action—an action, furthermore, that to be successful, cannot be negotiated, as it must be clandestine. The assumptions that speakers do adhere to the maxims must be relied on by deceivers, yet they have nothing to do with the occurrence of deceptive communication.

Now, does deception always involve a violation of the maxim of quality? Jacobs, Brashers, and Dawson (1996) and Jacobs, Dawson, and Brashers (1996) argue that even if other maxims are violated, for deception to occur there must be a quality violation in the form of a false implicature. If one agrees with the assumption that there must always be an implicature in the Gricean model, then the question the researchers pose must be answered positively, yet not in the way Jacobs, Dawson, and Brashers intended it. Such an implicature would necessarily have to be metadiscursive. In other words, it would convey something false about the deceptive utterance itself, that is, it would render it as cooperative. The only problem with the approach is that it assumes that any violation of a Gricean maxim must necessarily lead to deception, and this is always problematic. As I argued earlier, deception must involve manipulation of truth and falsity of propositions, and thus the maxim violation itself is not a sufficient condition in demarcating deceptive communication. This is indeed one significant problem with IMT itself.

Buller and Burgoon (1996a) criticize the Gricean approach on three fronts: first, for its imprecision (see also Thomas, 1995); second, for its weak empirical support; and, third, for the unclear role of all maxims in deception, which was discussed above. Finally, Buller and Burgoon (1996a) criticize IMT for not providing a full account of a deceptive interaction. The latter, however, is hardly justifiable, given that on the basis of Grice's theory, IMT cannot possibly claim to do it, necessarily focusing on the message itself.

One could, however, argue that Grice's theory is not a well-rounded account of human communication. Thomas (1995), for example, lists problems with intentionality of implicatures, types of nonobservance, and different nature of maxims and their overlap. Although acknowledging these problems, I would still like to argue that it is possible to take on the Gricean model as a heuristic schema for the analysis of deceptive communication. Even if their edges are "fuzzy," the maxims provide a useful and comprehensive account of how deception can occur. Furthermore, if seen as subject to relations of power or solidarity, as well as more fully contextualized within language activities and settings (Sarangi & Slembrouck, 1992), the cooperative principle can be regarded as a model referring to one of the most basic regulators of human communication.

Dismissing the studies testing IMT, Buller and Burgoon (1996a) point to their own showing that they support IDT and its predictions. Although that may well be the case, studies testing both IMT and IDT have one significant weakness in common. They are not attempts at analyzing naturally occurring deception. Rather, they both attempt to analyze *elicited* "deceptive" messages—that is, messages that participants *consider* to be deceptive, and this does not mean that they would actually use them in discourse in a natural setting.

The Gricean approach, however, has a weakness that cannot be easily overcome. Although providing a general framework within which to see deception, IMT cannot analyze the workings of a deceptive message, its structure, or pragmatic workings. In other words, if evasion and certain types of fallacies both violate the maxim of relation (e.g., Galasiński, 1996b), IMT would find it difficult to explain the differences between them (see also McCornack's [1997] critique). The Gricean approach must be complemented with a mechanism that allows distinguishing between various uncooperative communicative actions. Thus, in acknowledgment of the broad Gricean approach to deception—speakers violate, that is, unostentatiously break, maxims of conversation to mislead others—the next chapter attempts to provide answers to questions of how to analyze real-life deception and, furthermore, what type of messages people actually use in real life. In such a way, the next chapter is pivotal to this study. It introduces the discussion of my approach to the discourse analytical study of deceptive communication. It lays foundations for the discussion of deception in general, its various types, its theory, and its methodological grounding.

NOTE

1. One may also counterargue that the deceiver still wants to induce a false belief in the target regarding the nature of the initial utterance and what the deceiver intends to do with it. It seems, however, that the deceiver is counting on the preexisting—and false—assumptions as to the nature of the exchange that are held by the target. The target already assumes that the deceiver intends to deceive her or him and acts on such assumptions. These assumptions are a precondition of the deceiver's success.

Finally, this situation may also be argued to reinforce the target's false belief. If the target of a lying liar does infer the opposite of what the liar says, then the target reinforces her or his belief that the liar always lies. But in fact, the liar's actions are not aimed at reinforcing the belief. The liar, rather, counts on it, and the liar's utterance may indeed contribute to that, yet the aim is not to influence it.

3

How People Deceive

The bias toward studying leakage and detection in deception research has resulted in few programmatic studies of deception, and even fewer devoted to the analysis of the deceptive message itself. The theories of deceptive communication discussed in the previous chapter redress somewhat the lack of conceptualization, yet although attempting to construct general typologies of deceptive messages, they provide hardly any insight into the workings of the message itself. The typologies of deceptive message that they do offer are not based on clearly set criteria. Furthermore, the paucity of descriptions of the deceptive message is particularly acute with regard to linguistic studies (studies in Parret, 1994, are an exception and still do not provide a comprehensive account).

In addition, Miller and Stiff (1993; also McCornack, 1997) point out that deception research has suffered from not being based on the data acquired in natural settings. Difficulties in ascertaining whether a particular message is deceptive amount to the reasons why a majority of studies have drawn on messages generated in laboratories. This chapter aims to redress this state of affairs. I shall propose here a new approach to analyzing deception based on naturally occurring data and offer clear linguistic criteria for mapping out the types of deceptive actions.

Basic Assumptions

How does the analyst ascertain that a message is actually deceptive? Worse still, just how will she or he know whether a speaker did or did not intend to deceive? It is impossible to have empirical access to the deceptive intentions of the speaker. How does an analyst assess whether a speaker issues a false statement to induce a true belief, a false statement to induce a false belief, and so forth? The empirical inaccessibility of intentions or knowledge of deceivers leads to a conclusion that at least in part, deceptive communication cannot be empirically analyzed. It seems, however, that a partial solution is possible.

Let me first deal with the problem of falsity of utterances. The analyst of naturally occurring deceptive communication has to rely on *phenomenal* faculties of utterances. It is the utterance only that must provide clues to its deceptiveness, rather than, for example, either the deceiver's or the target's accounts of what happened. What the analyst has to look for in the data, therefore, is *misrepresentation* of reality. This is the only empirically accessible clue as to the *potential* aim with which the utterance has been issued. If this assumption is sound, the corpus of the data for studying deception in naturally occurring discourse will have to consist of utterances misrepresenting reality. I use the notion of misrepresentation broadly enough to encompass the gamut of deceptive uses—from straightforward lies/falsification, through half-truths, to deceptive implications. In such a way, I offer the notion of misrepresentation to include all those cases in which the utterance deviates from what the speaker believes to be a true account of the extralinguistic state of affairs. In itself, however, misrepresentation does not yet allow any excursions into the problem of whether it was or was not intended.

The issue of intentionality of deception can be reformulated as follows. The speakers may, on the one hand, have misrepresented reality intentionally and thus attempted to deceive the audience. On the other hand, the speakers may have either made a mistake or thought they were actually telling the truth. Either way, the analyst *does not know* which of the two is the case. I submit, however, that the way of dealing with the data is to assume that if the speakers did intend to misrepresent, they would have done it in the ways shown by the data. Thus, even if they misrepresented by accident, the data provide a valid insight into misrepresentation and thus into deception. There are, however, types of communicative activities (e.g., election debates) in which the speakers are more than likely to have additional strategic aims they want to achieve in the communicative encounter (cf., e.g., Benoit & Wells, 1996). Misrepresenting utterances in such cases and, more particularly, their rhetorical structures may indicate that the speakers must have intended to offer a preferred version of reality.

For all sorts of reasons, however, I wish to stress that I shall be making no claim whatsoever that the speakers whose utterances I shall be analyzing throughout the book did intend to deceive their addressees both in the immediate interaction and in the audience. My claim here is only that the patterns of their discourse can provide a useful insight into the analysis of deceptive communication, narrowed here to analyzing misrepresentation. This is also why, although it is, at times, impossible, I shall attempt not to reveal the speakers' identities—it is immaterial to my study.

As noted above, Miller and Stiff (1993), speaking of their regret of the paucity of natural-setting research, refer to the "obvious difficulties in ascertaining whether naturally occurring messages meet the criteria of deceptiveness" (p. 28). They do provide, however, some clues as to how researchers may tackle the problem. Investigative interviews, records of law enforcement agencies, and employment interviews are all nominated as potential sources of data for the analysis of deceptive communication. Still, Miller and Stiff draw attention to the never disappearing difficulty of assessing the veracity of the utterances. The difficulties Miller and Stiff point to are not likely to be overcome. At some point, the veracity assessment of claims in the data will require the researcher's knowledge of all the information relevant in a given context. It is highly unlikely that such a requirement could ever be met.

The ideal data for a deception researcher should therefore include two aspects:

1. The deceptive (misrepresenting) utterance

2. Data that provide access to the reality to which the deceptive message refers

Only then can it be argued that it is possible to assess the veracity of the speaker. I think it is possible to find this type of data. I shall analyze here the ways in which participants of debates *misrepresent contributions made by other debaters*. Because *both* the deceptive utterance and the reality it misrepresents are part of the debate, the problem described by Miller and Stiff (1993) disappears.

The proposed data may raise reservations that the deceptive message refers not to the extralinguistic reality but to another utterance. It seems, however, that there are no grounds for believing that the deceiver trying to misrepresent discourse will behave differently from the one who attempts to misrepresent nonlinguistic states of affairs. Moreover, it seems that the study of deception is tacitly based on this type of analysis. Misrepresentation implies a nontruthful as opposed to a truthful account of reality. It is, of course, only propositions that are truthful or false, and not reality itself. Deceivers misrepresent what they believe to be true accounts of a state of affairs and thus misrepresent more or less explicit propositions about reality.

The data will, however, also provide an opportunity for an insight into how users of language misrepresent discourse itself. I am not aware of any study that attempted to carry out such an analysis. This opportunity is also particularly important in the case of political discourse. Doing politics, it seems, predominantly consists of communicating.

DECEPTIVE STRATEGIES

The emphasis on linguistic data only also facilitates the design of the constructed typology. Every utterance in a dialogic (or polylogic) exchange projects a particular conversational demand (cf. Holdcroft, 1987; also Dascal, 1977) on the other interlocutor(s) in the exchange. It lays out a set of purposes with which it was issued. To be relevant, the other speaker has to meet the demand by performing a particular speech act. Now, Holdcroft (1987) argues that the conversational demand of an utterance can be construed as the propositional content of the utterance and its illocutionary force, or else a higher-order aim inferable from the context. The distinction can also be used in the context of analyzing misrepresentations of utterances. It seems that the goal of a deceptive speaker will be to misrepresent the conversational demand of the target utterance. Thus the deceptive speaker can target either the propositional content of the misrepresented contribution or its pragmatic functions—understood as the illocutionary force or a more global goal of the speaker (cf., e.g., Naughton & Craig, 1994). The typology proposed below will be based on the relationship that deceptive utterances have to the propositional content and the pragmatic functions of the target utterance.

The analysis of the data suggests that three types of misrepresentation are used in political debates. First are falsifications that consist of the deceiver's ascribing to another debater words that are in contradiction to what the debater actually said. Second are distortions, that is, representation of the claim made as stronger/more general or weaker/more particular. The third type can be described as "taking words out of context," that is, an element of the utterance is attributed a function different from the one it had in the original utterance. Obviously, the types distinguished here are not mutually exclusive and—as will be shown below—can and do occur together. The first two types are distinguished on the basis of the representation of the propositional content of the target utterance; the third type relates to the representation of the functions of the utterance (or its part).

Falsifications

The first type of strategies of misrepresenting debate contributions consists of falsely attributing a particular statement to a debater. The misrepresented utterance gives no grounds for representing it as the deceiver did. The deceiver can achieve this in two ways; he or she can leave some relationship between the two utterances or not. The relationship is such that the deceptive speaker attempts to construct her or his utterance operating within the same knowledge frame (cf. Sanders, 1987; also Brown & Yule, 1983) as that of the original speaker. In such a way, the deceiver may give the impression that he or she is actually talking about the same thing. This in turn may convince the audience that the speaker is actually making a justified interpretation of what was originally said. Utterances of this type are used in two strategies: (a) manipulation of the participants involved in the processes represented in the target utterance and (b) manipulation of the processes themselves (for the distinction of participants and processes, cf. Halliday, 1994; also Simpson, 1993).

Let me first deal with those misrepresentations in which no relationship between the target utterance (i.e., the misrepresented one) and the misrepresenting one exists. Consider the following examples.[1]

(1)

A: How can we create high-paying jobs with the education system we have? And what would you do to change it?

B: What should we do? Let me reel some things off 'cause you said you wanted specifics. . . .

(2)

A: The difficulty he's got is that whatever the outcome, he won't have dealt with the divisions in his party. That's why I think it's a desperate short-term gesture, because the fault lines are there: on Europe, on health service, on privatization, on Nolan, across the board—are so strong. Unless he tackles these, he's not gonna offer the country what it wants—which is leadership, a sense of purpose, . . . and Labour, the New Labour, would offer them that sense of purpose.

B: [John Major tries] to put behind the party for the good of the country the divisions which are there. [A] is quite right. There are divisions about Europe. . . . For her to say that New Labour is not divided on Europe, they are just as divided as we are.

In (1), B, a U.S. presidential candidate, ascribes the nonexistent demand to the questioner and in such a way not only enables himself to include details of his own ideas but also can present himself as a person who is willing to answer the question and who caters to the needs of the potential voter. In the case of (2)—where A, a member of the Labour shadow cabinet, refers to John Major's handling of the leadership challenge of 1995—B, a member of the Tory cabinet, in an attempt to save the image of his party, ascribes to his interlocutor words that she had not uttered. A makes no claim as to the unity of her party on the European issues (although one could argue that by contrasting the two parties, she implies New Labour's unity on the matter).

Manipulating the Participants

Speakers also attempt to preserve a relationship between their utterances and the misrepresented ones. The first strategy they employ consists of focusing on the participants involved in the processes represented in the utterance. The misrepresentation concerns *who* or *what* is referred to in the utterance. The processes referred to remain more or less unchanged. Witness the following examples (A and C are presidential candidates, B is the moderator).

(3)

A1: Probably we are making a mistake night after night after night to cast the nation's future on a unit so small.

B: Why is it a mistake?

A2: It's irrelevant. What he did as the governor of Arkansas is irrelevant. . . . You know, I could say that I ran a small grocery store on the corner, therefore I extrapolate that on the fact that I can run [*inaudible*]. That's not true.

C: I am frankly amazed that since you grew up five blocks from there, you would think that what goes on in that state is irrelevant. I think it's been pretty impressive.

C claims that A declared the events in Arkansas as irrelevant. A indeed spoke of irrelevance, yet of the irrelevance of C's experience, rather than the said events. Such claims from A, of course, have to be countered by C—the former questions the latter's fitness to become president. Moreover, C's misrepresentation could have achieved one more goal—representing A as someone who does not care about local issues. At least some of the inhabitants of Arkansas might not have liked that what happened in their state was described as irrelevant.

Witness also:

(4)

A: They also felt that it wasn't the right time to make the change [homosexuals' rights to join the armed forces], and I would agree with that.

B: I'm always suspicious of ministers who say that . . . now is not the time for that. It's always the time for argument and discussion.

(5)

A: John Major has been undermined by a few people who have been sniping away—some privately, some semipublicly—and if we don't slake the boil . . . then this state of uncertainty will go on. What he's done for this country's sake and for our party's sake is [he] said, "Let's have it out now, back me or sack me, put up or shut up."

B: Well, this is quite wrong, Michael, for you to suggest that a very small number of us who were deprived of the whip have such a potent influence in the country—

A: ⎡I am not saying that you have.

B: ⎣—that we are responsible for the current position of the Conservative Party and the polls.

In (4), B, a church minister, ascribes to A, a member of the Conservative cabinet, what in fact was said by somebody else. (5), on the other hand, contains at least two misrepresentations. The one pertinent here is that A, a member of the Conservative cabinet, does not specify the group of people attacking the prime minister. B, a controversial Tory member of Parliament, however, declares that A's words refer to "us"—a group of Tory rebels whose parliamentary whip was withdrawn. The other misrepresentation—the construction of A's utterance as placing the group in question as responsible for the state of the Conservatives—allows B to criticize (indirectly at least) John Major and the Conservatives' executive. The misfortunes of the party are implied to be shared by others (presumably the Tories' management) than the group in question.

Manipulating the Processes

The speaker trying to retain some relationship between her or his misrepresentation and the target utterance may also attempt to manipulate the process in the propositional content of the target. While maintaining *who* or *what* is referred to in the utterance, the speaker this time tries to misrepresent *how* they are referred to, or what is told about them. Witness:

(6)

A: To some extent, teachers have played with fire themselves. There's been a deliberate reduction of the gap between the teacher and the taught. . . . I think the teacher-pupil relationship needs a certain formality. Formality does have a use. And what we are doing is producing an unstructured society, and in an unstructured society, violence flourishes very easily. Teachers, I think, shouldn't only attack their pupils, they should look at themselves, their methods, the language they themselves use.

B: I think it's a disgrace for [A] to suggest that if a teacher is attacked, it's the teacher's own fault.

(7)

A: This issue of the single European currency . . . this is a highly technical complex issue. You need highly technical qualified advice on what we should or shouldn't be doing and that is not for me a subject for a referendum.

B: I resent being told that the society isn't intelligent enough to grasp these issues. That is an excuse not to have a referendum, that is a reason for educating people.

A: I didn't say, I didn't make the point that the country isn't intelligent enough. I think that there are issues when you do go off and seek advice.

In (6), A, a British academic, focuses his propositions on teachers and on what they should or should not do. B, a Labour shadow minister, however, attributes to him the claim that teachers are themselves responsible for attacks on them. A can be seen to blame teachers for the lack of formality, for producing an unstructured society. Yet when he speaks of violence, there is no direct attribution of blame to them. In her misrepresentation, B uses the possible interpretation that A was indeed blaming but focuses on a different kind of blame. A similar situation occurs in the case of (7), where A, a Labour shadow minister, makes a point of seeking advice, while B, a member of the audience, chooses to interpret it as a statement about the society's intellectual abilities.

Distortions

In contrast to falsifications, distortions are all those utterances in which the speaker not so much lies but exaggerates, overstates, or minimalizes. Distortions consist in changing the strength or scope of the propositions made in the misrepresented utterance. Target utterances are represented as stronger/more general or weaker/more particular than those that were actually made.

Stronger Claims

The largest group in the corpus are utterances in which speakers augmented claims made by other debaters. Such misrepresentations can take a number of forms: For example, if a predicate in a proposition is replaced by another that shows more commitment, this increases the degree of obtaining of certain conditions. Alternatively, deceptive speakers represented propositions as if they applied more widely or to a larger number of cases, and so forth.

Consider the following examples. (8) was part of a debate whether the European Union in general and the United Kingdom in particular should attempt to influence Russia to stop the atrocities committed by the Russian troops on the Chechen population. The issue became a controversial one, and this is how B, a Tory cabinet minister, handled the debate:

(8)

A: We have no right to interfere in Russian internal politics.

B: In a narrow sense, I agree with what the gentleman in the audience said. We cannot intervene. It's not our direct responsibility.

By changing *interfering* to *intervening,* B achieves a relatively uncontroversial footing. Although it is possible to argue that interfering, for example, by applying political pressure on Russia, is possible and perhaps feasible, an intervention (with all its connotations of an abrupt, drastic, and possibly military action) is not. B therefore does not have to indicate his views on the problem of interfering; he makes his views known with regard to intervention. Moreover, by means of (falsely) constructing his utterance as an agreement, B manages also to indicate that he merely takes up an earlier point and thus that his views are not isolated. It is also noteworthy that B introduces his utterance by a hedge ("in a narrow sense").[2]

B's utterance with regard to it is problematic. At first sight, the hedge seems to indicate that the act performed is an agreement but only in a narrow sense. Such a formulation, however, hardly makes sense—one cannot agree in a broad or narrow sense (although one can agree broadly). Instead, the hedge seems to modify the verb *interfere* used by A. B agrees with noninterfering in a narrow sense, with the exception that he changes it to intervening. The hedge is on the Gricean maxim of quality; it signals to the addressee that to be truthful, B must make a reservation on what he agrees with. Thus, B not only softens his stronger (*sic!*) claim, he also indicates that he is willing to be truthful, accurate, and so on, whereas in fact he is not. The hedge is used as a device licensing a potential inaccuracy (Mura, 1983), except that in the case of (8), the inaccuracy is actual.

Consider also:

(9)

A: M.P.s should be dedicated to their constituency to being a member of Parliament.

B: I do agree particularly with the last speaker who said that M.P.s should be dedicated and loyal to those who placed them in position.

In (9), B, a Tory member of Parliament, adds loyalty to the proposition made by A, strengthening the claim made earlier. The goal B tries to achieve with his misrepresentation is likely to be a negative presentation of one of the debaters, a former Conservative M.P. who crossed the floor of the House of Commons and joined one of the opposition parties. The move, of course, was decried by the Tories.

Consider now:

(10)

A: We all agree, and evidence suggests, that we are right to agree that marriage remains the cornerstone of a good society. Children from divorced parents, and I am one of them, are that much more likely to become juvenile delinquents, are that much more likely to do badly at school, are that much more likely to be part of this truancy group.

B: It is wrong to imply that single parents all bring up people who are juvenile delinquents, people who are truantries—

A: —I never implied that.

B: Well it is—

A: —Hold on a second.

[*B continues without paying attention.*]

(11)

A: I believe that a lot of the Conservative party have already written off the next election. Some of them are actually hoping to lose the next election so they can go into [*inaudible*] opposition, regroup, and come back with a new purest philosophy.

B: For [A] to say that Conservatives have written off the next election—he really doesn't understand much about history. That's what people were saying in 1992, and look what happened there.

There are two ways in which B, a Tory M.P. known for her right-wing views, attempts to manipulate the representation of A's utterance in (10). First, she falsely ascribes to her the claim about single parents, and second, she presents A's claim as referring to *all* children in question, whereas in fact A claimed only their likelihood to become something. Interestingly, B chooses to construct A's claims as implied, rather than asserted. Admittedly, it functions as a possible safety net in the case of a protestation. Still, when the protestation does come, B pays little attention to it and does not give up her turn, leaving A visibly distressed.

Also in (11), B, a Tory politician, presents A's (a Liberal Democrat M.P.) claim as more general. He presents A as referring to the Tory party in general, whereas A was speaking of *a lot of* the party. B's misrepresentation could be used not only to undermine the speaker but also to undermine his claim and render it unlikely to be true. The misrepresented claim refers to all the Tories— thus also to B himself—whereas B presents himself as one who has not written off the next election. B is the live evidence of the falsity of A's claim.

Weaker Claims

In contrast to the group of utterances just discussed, the utterances analyzed below play down the claims made in misrepresented utterances or represent them as having a narrower scope. Thus, the target utterance will get represented as referring to only part or an aspect of the state of affairs in question. Consider first:

(12)

A: I think we have to do everything that we possibly can to both deter young people from taking drugs and experimenting with drugs. And the young people themselves have to take some responsibility. Parents have got to, people like ourselves . . . have got to. But the other thing is that the government has to take much more action than they have been taking . . . because parents can't stop drugs being transported round the world or brought to this country.

B: I think it would be great if it was only a story of clamping down on supply as [A] was mentioning.

B, a Tory minister, putting what was said by A, a Labour politician, into the presupposition—and thus taking for granted that his representation is truthful—chooses to omit the argument about individuals' responsibilities. A now is presented as making a (simplistic) claim that taking care of the drug problem is merely the question of supply. Note also that in his response, B focuses on the criticism of the government made by A. By undermining A's claims and implying their simplicity, B at the same time plays down the importance of the issue (clamping down on the drug supply) and thus undermines the criticism itself and avoids the possibility of being put in the negative light.

Consider now:

(13)

A: Can you imagine what effect this [Princess Diana's 1994 BBC interview] must have on her sons—the two boys sitting there watching her admit adultery not only on nationwide television but on worldwide television. Now if there are any problems in my family, they're not gonna be broadcast on "Panorama."

B: I agree on the last point on the effects on the children and that it wasn't helpful to them.

In this case, B represents A's damning implications that the Princess of Wales's interview must have had very negative effects on her children as "unhelpful." It is noteworthy that B does not explicitly claim that A did actually say that. The relationship of misrepresentation is established by the initial phrase of B's utterance: *I agree.* The act of agreeing implies that the speaker does not alter what she or he agrees with. Arguably, B employs here a means of concealing the misrepresentation, a matter I shall discuss in detail in Chapter 5.

But B may be simply trying to paraphrase A's words politely. She tries to avoid expressing extreme emotions, and so on, and thus the problem of misrepresentation does not arise. The problem with such an argument, however, is that B clearly ascribes the "polite" expression to A, who had earlier declared his republican views (an admission rarely made by a member of the British Parliament). Thus, B misrepresented A's utterance, avoiding thereby a debate on the monarchy while being able to express her sympathy toward the Princess's sons. Instead of appearing to agree with extreme views on a member of the Royal family, B, by misrepresenting, could agree with moderate ones.

Consider now:

(14)

A: There are lucky politicians and unlucky politicians. Norman Lamont was an unlucky politician. Is that what you really mean by refreshing the government? To have a lucky man like Kenneth Clarke running the treasury?

B: It's certainly not what I mean. You're quite right to say, of course, that Norman Lamont has been chancellor of the Exchequer during a particularly difficult period and has tackled some very difficult problems. I think in a way that has produced some very important problems.

(15)

A: We don't have good trade agreements across the world.

B: [A] says it's a bad deal [the NAFTA], Mr. Bush says it's a hunky-dory deal. I say, on balance, it does more good than harm, if we can get some protection for the environment so Mexicans have to follow their own environmental standards, their own labor law standards, and if we have a genuine commitment to reeducate and reform the American workers who lose their jobs and reinvest in this economy. I have a realistic approach to this agreement. . . . I know there are good things about this agreement, but it sure can be made better.

The overall claim about a politician in A's utterance in (14) gets represented by a fellow cabinet member as a claim referring only to a number of problems that faced the chancellor of the Exchequer in this particular capacity. On the other hand, in (15), A's general statement is misrepresented by a U.S. presidential countercandidate as referring to only one particular trade agreement.

Taking Words Out of Context

The final type of misrepresentations used in political debates is what I called "taking words out of context." The deceptive speaker presents what was actually said yet attributes to the utterance or its part a different pragmatic function from the one it originally had. The deceiver imposes a certain interpretation of a contribution to a debate, an interpretation that is not warranted by the linguistic evidence. Consider the following examples in which speakers B take up an element of A's utterance and misrepresent its original use.

(16)

A: They've [Tories] put taxes up year on year by the equivalent of 7p in a pound. . . . Because they're under pressure, because of their broken promises, they've given 1p of that 7p increase back. But at the same time as giving the 1p back, they've actually taken it away again with a higher council tax, a higher price of petrol. . . .

B: The problem for [A] with the very smart 7p-1p slogan is this: Does that mean that she would want to cut taxes even more?

(17)

A: Do you agree that if the country adopts the single currency, it must inevitably lead to a federal Europe dominated by Germany with Parliament's power being reduced to a parish council?

B: If we have a single currency, that gentleman over there is dead right. Everything will be transferred to some central bank in Germany, and we will become a county council.

Thus, in (16), while, admittedly, A, the shadow Labour minister, attempts to argue her case by means of referring to numbers, B presents the use of numbers as a slogan. Such a label may well undermine the utterance's credibility. In (17), the claim that a single currency will shift the center of power to Germany is put by A, member of the audience, into his question and is not asserted, as B presents it ("that gentleman . . . is dead right"). She also presents his claim as stronger than in fact was made—while A speaks of Germany dominating Europe, B chooses to speak of a central bank in Germany having all the power. It is noteworthy that B is a Euro-sceptic M.P.—what she achieves, therefore, is a presentation of a potential voter as sympathetic to her views.

A somewhat different action is taken by B in (18) and (19), in which B declares what type of intentions A had when making his contribution to the discussion. Consider:

(18)

A: I would like to ask [B] a question. . . . How much of all this extra money you keep talking about that has gone into NHS [National Health Service] over the last 2 or 3 years has actually had to be spent on banks of computers and all the other [*inaudible*] to introduce your rather complicated accounting system, because my impression is that a heck of a lot.

B: What you heard was all prejudice against managers, computers, and all those sorts of things.

(19)

A: Mr. Perot says it's a bad deal [the NAFTA], B says it's a hunky-dory deal. I say, on balance, it does more good than harm, if we can get some protection for the environment so Mexicans have to follow their own environmental standards, their own labor law standards, and if we have a genuine commitment to reeducate and reform the American workers who lose their jobs and reinvest in this economy. I have a realistic approach to this agreement. . . . I know there are good things about this agreement, but it sure can be made better.

B: I think he's made my case. On the one hand, it's a good agreement; on the other, I'll make it better. Right now we heard it. Ross is against, I am for it. *He* says, "On the one hand I am for it, just on the other, I may be against."

In (18), A and B are political opponents, and thus A is likely to want to score points at B's expense. But the utterance of B, member of the Conservative cabinet, is hardly justifiable on the grounds of what A said. A can easily be seen to be indirectly arguing against an expensive accounting system. B's strategy is interesting. B does not want to give an answer to A's question and evades it. B, however, also attempts to justify her evasion—precisely by referring to A's utterance as prejudice. After all, prejudice does not merit a rational discussion.

In (19), A's utterance misrepresenting an earlier one (see [15] above) gets misrepresented in the reaction it elicited. A uses his misrepresentation to present himself as a moderate, reasoned politician, one who can rationally evaluate reality and knows that there are no ideal agreements. This particular tactic is misrepresented as a declaration of indecisiveness. One could argue that B tries to present A's utterance as an expressive speech act, a confession of hesitations, uncertainty, and so on. B's utterance is used in an attempt to present A in negative terms, as someone who cannot make up his mind. Although A situates himself in opposition to the other two participants of the debate and thus tries to stress his uniqueness, B's tactic is to show the candidate that he is likely to have considered the main opponent in running for office as different from him and the other candidate. They both can make up their minds; A cannot. In the two utterances (A's and B's, respectively), uniqueness is used as both a positive and a negative value.

In the following two exchanges, misrepresenting speakers construe the target utterance as a particular speech act. Speakers B in (20) and in (21) are different persons reacting to the same utterance.

(20)

A: I don't think we will ever win with Saddam Hussein. I guess in the end, an assassin's bullet will get him.

B: Do I hear a churchwoman urging to go out and assassinate Saddam Hussein?

A: I don't think I exactly said that.

(21)

A: I don't think we will ever win with Saddam Hussein. I guess in the end, an assassin's bullet will get him.

B: I think [A] came closest perhaps to suggesting it that the only solution is to go in and to take Saddam Hussein out dead or alive, that's the only solution.

A: I didn't say that.

In (20), B constructs A's utterance as a directive speech act, that is, attempting to get something done, whereas in fact it is groundless to do so. A makes a statement or a prediction of the likely death of Saddam Hussein. For the utterance to count as urging, A would have to try to get somebody to do the killing. No such agent either explicitly or implicitly is present in the structure of the utterance. One could argue here, of course, that because the claim of urging is put into question, it does not have the full power of skewing the represented reality. Still, despite A's protest, her utterance was interpreted similarly in (21) only a few minutes after the exchange. Similarly, also in (21), a statement on the likely fate of Saddam Hussein is represented as coming close to suggesting a solution and thus as a directive, rather than an assertive, speech act. B attempts to safeguard himself against the possible challenge. He chooses to construct the target utterance as both "came closest" and merely suggesting the solution—admittedly, an indirect way of rendering a directive.

In summary, I have argued that there are three main types of misrepresentation: falsifications, distortions, and taking words out of context. The first two types focus on the propositional content of the target utterances, the third on their pragmatic functions.

Implicit Misrepresentations

A survey of literature (e.g., Buller & Burgoon, 1994; Galasiński, 1994a) suggests that a number of studies dealing with typologies of deceptive messages include implied information as one of the types of deceptive action, on a par with exaggerations, minimalizations, and others. I argue, however, that misrepresentations carried by the utterances implicitly are no different from those that were discussed above. Implications—whether implicatures or presuppositions—are not distinct types of deceptive strategies. Consider the following examples.

(22)

   A: Now I can get rid of it [the budget deficit] in 4 years, in theory, on the books now, but to do it, you'd have to raise taxes too much and cut the benefits to the people who need them, and it would even make the economy worse. . . . [You need to] ask the wealthiest Americans and foreign corporations to pay their share in taxes.

   B: I am a little confused here because I don't see how you can grow the deficit down by raising people's taxes. Let's not raise taxes on the American people now. I just don't believe that would stimulate any kind of growth at all.

(23)

   A: I applaud the government's initiative in moving particularly in my area of mental health in actually planning mental health as one of its five major objectives.

   B: I was very pleased to hear [A] say that she in principle at least applauded the direction of the policy.

In the case of (22), an excerpt from a U.S. presidential debate, B implies that A wants to raise taxes. He flouts the maxim of manner because of the overt ambiguity of the *us* ("Let's") in the second sentence and thereby the maxim of relation—the part of the utterance becomes irrelevant because there is no one who might count as its addressee. In (23), the misrepresentation is rendered by two presuppositions—the first introduced by the initial clause "I was very pleased to hear," and the other by the verb *say.* In such a way, the speaker takes as given, something not to be disputed, what he says next. B presupposes that what he says that A said is true, and that she actually did applaud the direction of the government's policy. In fact, his utterance misrepresents A's applauding of the government's priorities as the applauding of the direction of a specific policy. Interestingly, *applaud* was actually used by A, and thus B manages to use it as a means of concealing the misrepresentation.

If my analysis is correct in that the misrepresentations in (22) and (23) are falsifications akin to those discussed in the previous sections of this chapter, then there is no point in creating another classification category for implied misrepresentations. The typology of deceptive actions described earlier does not have to be extended.

In Chapter 5, I shall also argue that implicit misrepresentations belong to the realm of *metadiscursive deception,* that is, all those situations in which the speaker targets her or his own deceptive message trying to present it as something different from what it actually is.

MISREPRESENTATION OR DECEPTION: THE PROBLEM REVISITED

At the beginning of this chapter, I said that there is no easy solution to the problem of deciding whether the speaker misrepresented by mistake, by accident, or intentionally. As there is no empirical access to the speaker's intention, the analyst cannot know for sure which is the case—mistake or deception. Admittedly, the method of asking for speakers' reports, especially in the case of public figures, is unlikely to bring encouraging results.

Yet on the analysis of the data, one could, in my opinion, claim that it is possible to have an "informed guess" about what the speaker wanted to achieve with a message. Consider now (24), in which A is a business journalist and B is a member of the Tory government that had just announced its budget.

(24)

A: The reason I object to the budget . . . is that I don't actually think the treasury has based its assumptions on the right forecasts. I don't think we're gonna have 3% growth.

B: Sue has put her finger on what of course can push this budget out or any other budget, for that matter. If there is a serious recession in our export market or we don't get reasonable growth, then we or Labour or anybody else who is in power would face [*inaudible*].

One of the misrepresentations in B's utterance is the shift from the assumptions that make the budget objectionable to future factors that may result in the budget's nonviability. The shift, therefore, is one from an error of judgment to the unpredictability of the future.

Now, given that B is a secretary of state, the assumption that he simply accidentally misrepresented A's utterance to his gain would be implausible. One must assume that B will do his best to show himself and the government in the most positive way and will be particularly vigilant when the government is criticized, especially in view of the government's losing in opinion polls to the main opposition party. Although certainly possible, an accident or a mistake is unlikely. B's misrepresentation serves his political goal. And although this claim is still far from ascribing an intention to mislead to B, his utterance can be analyzed as serving the overarching strategy of positive self-presentation.

Now, I have made the claims of the political expediency of misrepresentations often throughout this chapter. Time and again, it was possible to see how a misrepresentation serves the speaker or could have served the goal of negative presentation of the political opponent. Misrepresentation that can be seen as a repeated communicative activity and serving clear and desirable goals cannot be assessed as chance—be it mistakes or false beliefs of the one who represents. The only possible conclusion for the researcher is that at least those misrepresentations must have been intended where it was possible to infer the expediency for the speaker by drawing on the context.

CONCLUDING REMARKS

I set two objectives for this chapter. On the one hand, I wanted to offer solutions to some methodological problems in the study of deception; on the other, the chapter presents a typology of deceptive actions based on naturally occurring data.

A researcher of deceptive communication will face two main problems. First, there is the problem of studying deception in its natural context, focusing on unsolicited data; second, there is the problem of assessing the deceptiveness of the utterance. I have argued that studying debates and how debaters misrepresent others' contributions provides a rich resource for such data. One thus achieves access to both the deceptive message and the reality to which it refers. Unfortunately, the focus for the research must be only one aspect of deceptive communication (although probably the most important and typical)—misrepresentation.

I have distinguished between three main types of misrepresentations: falsifications, distortions, and taking words out of context. The distinction between the three types is that the first two rely on misrepresenting the propositional content of the target utterance, whereas the third focuses on its pragmatic functions.

I would like to argue that there are two main advantages with the typology proposed here. First, it offers clear criteria of classification of deceptive messages. The explicitness of basing the typology on the relationship between utterances has made it easier to arrive at such distinguishing criteria. Second, the typology is enriched by the inclusion of the category of taking words out of context. Although interested in how deceptive messages misrepresent nonlinguistic reality, researchers of deception have not paid attention to the fact that words also can be misrepresented. The category in question seems to be a distinct set of utterances that was not described earlier.

The next two chapters shift the perspective of this book. They will deal with what I have called *metadiscursive deception*. I shall now be interested in how speakers attempt to misrepresent what they themselves are saying.

NOTES

1. Quoting from the corpus, I shall always provide first the utterance that is the object of misrepresentation (target) and then the misrepresenting one. It is important to remember, however, that in some cases, the two utterances were not adjacent in the debate and

may have been separated by other contributions. The transcription of the data is limited to the minimum necessary for the purpose of the analysis.

2. Brown and Levinson (1987) define *hedges* as particles, words, or phrases that modify the degree of membership of a predicate or noun phrase in a set. They say of that membership that it is partial, or true only in certain respects, or that it is more true and complete than might be expected. Such expressions as *a sort of, rather,* and *technically* (as in "Technically, it is linguistics") are referred to as hedges. Brown and Levinson distinguish also between hedges on the illocutionary force and hedges on Gricean maxims of conversation. The former include expressions such as *really* ("He really did run away"), *sincerely, I wonder,* and question tags. The latter include, for example, mental verbs (*I think, I believe, I suppose*) and expressions such as *roughly, approximately, more or less,* and others.

4

Deceptiveness of Evasion

The idea that evasion is a deceptive strategy is commonplace in the literature on deception (see Bradac, 1983; Bradac et al., 1986; Ekman, 1985; Hopper & Bell, 1984; Gibbons, Bradac, & Busch, 1992; Knapp & Vangelisti, 1992; Metts, 1989; Ng & Bradac, 1993). It is founded on the assumption that evasive messages are a means of avoiding telling the truth, or, in other words, withholding a piece of truthful and relevant information. In this chapter, I shall examine the deceptiveness of evasion. I want to answer the question of whether evasive utterances should, and if so, how, they can be conceptualized as a type of deceptive communication.

I shall begin with the question of how to define evasion. This issue is rarely addressed, and there is little overlap between the different definitions offered (cf., e.g., Dillon, 1990; Harris, 1991; Ng & Bradac, 1993; Orr & Burkins, 1976). Consequently, I shall attempt to distinguish between different types of evasive messages. Finally, the typology will be used as a frame of reference in my considerations of evasion with regard to its deceptiveness.

WHAT IS EVASION?

Although often referred to in the literature on deception, evasion has so far merited relatively little attention from researchers. Moreover, the concept of evasion is more often than not treated intuitively without adequate conceptualization (cf. Ekman, 1985; Gibbons et al., 1992; Knapp & Vangelisti, 1992). Orr and Burkins (1976) suggest that evasion has to do with equivocation and ambiguity (cf. also Bull, 1994). Dillon (1990) sees evasion as nonanswer responses, those that relate coherently to the act of questioning yet not to the question-sentence. An evasive message then, according to Dillon, is an interactional move, rather than a sentence. One can infer from what Harris (1991) writes that a response is

55

evasive if (a) it doesn't answer the question directly or (b) it challenges the question.

Evasion receives more comprehensive treatment in the work of Bradac (1983), who sees evasion as covering all the ground referred to separately above. Bradac proposes that evasions are messages that the speaker believes will fail to inform the addressee about a relevant belief A or will inform the addressee of matters other than A (see also Bull & Mayer, 1993). Recently, this approach has been amended. Ng and Bradac (1993) argue that evasive messages are those intended as irrelevant and—to add a further qualification—that can be interpreted unambiguously. The Ng and Bradac definition introduces the notion of intention in the description of evasion. First, it is necessary to make a distinction between irrelevance in general and irrelevance that can count as evasion. An interlocutor who does not realize that he or she is making an irrelevant remark (e.g., after failing to understand a question) cannot, of course, be held responsible for evasion. One cannot evade and not realize it. Second, not all intended irrelevance counts as evasion. An irrelevant remark—made to make interlocutors laugh or to disrupt the conversation—is not evasive, merely because there is nothing to evade. Evasion pertains to the realm of question-answer exchanges.

That said, evasion can probably occur in situations with a nonlinguistic equivalent of a question, as in the cases of expectations set by the regular contextual features. Take, for example, the case of a spouse's coming home late. The need to account for the lateness may lead to evasion without a question being asked (I owe the point and the example to U. H. Meinhof). I argue that the nature of the evasive action does not change in such contexts. That the question remains implicit does not alter that it may be answered and, consequently, evaded. The same argumentation applies, in my view, to follow-ups in question-answer exchanges, except that here, evaders will actually evade a question that had originally been asked.

On the other hand, such communicative actions as qualifications are not evasions, unless they are part of an answer. Qualifications may well safeguard speakers from committing themselves to a particular statement, but that is not yet evasion. Otherwise, actions such as hedges would have to be incorporated into the category, which does not seem plausible.

Consider now three exchanges in view of the definition offered by Ng and Bradac (1993).

(1)

A: How has the national debt personally affected each of you?

B: I think the national debt affects everybody. Obviously, it has a lot to do with interest rates.

(2)

A: You say that the government is weak. Is the prime minister weak, too?

B: I refuse to make this kind of judgments. [*translated from Polish*]

(3)

A: Do you think that it is true?

B: I'd like to just talk about issues.

I submit that the responses to the questions in (1) through (3) are evasive. None of the respondents answers the question satisfying the demand for information posed by the questioner (cf. Bull & Mayer, 1993). In (1)—an exchange between a member of the audience and a U.S. presidential candidate—B's utterance contains a proposition that is too general to count as a cooperative answer. In the case of (2), the answerer openly refuses to answer A's question—a behavior described by Grice (1975) as opting out of cooperation. Finally, the response in (3)—another excerpt from a U.S. presidential debate—is an open attempt to control the topical content of the exchange, possibly implying (by flouting the maxim of relation) that B is unwilling to answer the question and does not consider the problem as belonging to the topical domain within which he wishes to operate.

Although all three responses are evasive, only the response in (1) can be counted as irrelevant to the question posed; the other two seem relevant—albeit in different ways. Saying that one will not answer a question—as in (2)—is, by definition, a relevant response. The same applies to the response in (3). The answer refers, although indirectly, to the question it is a response to. Both can be seen as relevant—they are contributions to the progression of the sequence toward an outcome (see Sanders, 1987). Furthermore, Gorayska and Lindsay (1993) point out that relevance is a relation that presupposes the existence of a goal (see also Hitchcock, 1992), that is, something is relevant to someone who seeks to achieve a goal. Thus, the utterances in question are relevant. They address the questioner's goal of getting some information from B—the responses in (2) and (3) render that goal unachievable. The problem, it seems, is what is meant by relevance.

Relevance and Evasion

Relevance became a crucial issue in the study of language and communication after it was included as one of the main factors governing our communication. In his theory of the cooperative principle, Grice (1975) argued that for interlocutors to be cooperative, they have to adhere to, among other things, the maxim of relation—the utterance must be relevant (for accounts of Grice's theory, see, e.g., Levinson, 1983; Mey, 1993; Schiffrin, 1994; Thomas, 1995). Grice did not make it clear, however, what he meant by saying that a communicator should be relevant.

Dascal (1977) and Holdcroft (1987) propose that utterance X is relevant to utterance Y if the former meets the conversational demand of the latter. Conversational demand, in turn, is understood (Holdcroft, 1987) as an illocutionary act whose determinants are its illocutionary force (e.g., that of ordering, promising, and apologizing) and its propositional content (what is actually ordered, promised, or apologized for). It can also be extended to some higher aim in discourse. It follows from such a formulation that there are two main types of relevance—pragmatic and semantic. Pragmatic relevance is a relation of two speech acts. Utterance X is pragmatically relevant if it pragmatically meets the conversational demand of utterance Y. To do this, utterance X must have an appropriate force or in some other way refer to the achievement of the goals set by utterance Y. Semantic relevance, on the other hand, is a relation between the propositional contents of utterances. Utterance X is semantically relevant to utterance Y if its proposition meets the conversational demand of the proposition in Y. Dascal (1977), speaking of semantic relevance, refers to such notions as reference, "aboutness," meaning relations. Sanders (1987), on the other hand, considers propositional contents relevant to each other if they are about components in the same knowledge structure.

It can be concluded from these approximations that the responses in (2) and (3) are only pragmatically relevant. As I pointed out earlier, they contribute to the progression of discourse; their speakers operate within the framework of the goal set out by the questioner. Both utterances, however, are not relevant in the semantic understanding of the word because neither is a response to the questions posed. The question in

(2)

A: You're saying that the government is weak. Is the prime minister weak, too?

demands an answer referring to the answerer's view on the position of the prime minister. More specifically, the question demands either "yes" or "no" as the answer. The response in

(2)

B: I refuse to make this kind of judgments. [*translated from Polish*]

does neither. Furthermore, it even fails to make a direct reference to the demanded state of affairs in the extralinguistic reality. The same applies to the exchange in (3). The response fails to address the issue of what the answerer thinks of the truth of a particular claim.

Consider another, somewhat more complicated, example here.

(4)

A1: They tell me that you've risen in the betting to be the next chancellor of the Exchequer.

B1: We've got an excellent chancellor of the Exchequer, very unfairly criticized. He's been laying foundations for the prospect, the exciting prospect I've been talking about.

A2: But when he is finished, you will take over?

B2: We've got an excellent chancellor of the Exchequer. I expect him to be there for a long time.

Both B's responses are relevant pragmatically. A wants to know whether his interlocutor, a member of the Tory government, is going to be the next chancellor of the Exchequer. Saying that the current chancellor of the Exchequer is excellent, B, as it were, wants to preempt any further discussion on the topic (in addition to putting himself in a good light). There is no point in discussing the matter—the post is occupied. B, however, is also evasive. It is difficult to pinpoint exactly the conversational demand of A1 because it is not a question syntactically. Through its pragmatics, however, the interlocutor infers that A1 demands an answer at least of the sort "Yes, I am the next candidate" or the like, with B referring to himself in relation to the office of the chancellor of the Exchequer. B fails to do so by referring to the actual person and thus is semantically irrelevant, pretending, however, otherwise. The second part of the exchange is much more straightforward. A2's response is a question that can be answered by "yes" or "no." B2's response is neither of them; semantically, it does not respond to the question.

Definition of Evasion

I think that semantic irrelevance is universal in acts of evasion. The modification of the definition put forward by Ng and Bradac (1993) must consist precisely in distinguishing between semantic and pragmatic relevance. *Evasive utterances are those that are intended to be semantically irrelevant.* I take this definition to encompass cases that imply the structure of the question by their intonation, phrasing, and quickness of response (see Bavelas et al., 1990a). Thus, if the question is "How did I do?" and the answer is "Really well!" I assume that the answer is semantically relevant. This definition also covers evasive utterances made in response to indirect questions. If the question is "Why is he still in the White House?" the speaker does not expect the addressee to answer "because I have confidence in him" (example quoted in Naughton & Craig, 1994)—which is semantically relevant, yet evasive with regard to the implied point concerning X's fitness for his office. The definition I propose can be retained with a reservation that in the case of implied questions, semantic relevance should be understood as the relevance to the implication, rather than to the literal question.

COVERT EVASION

Consider now the following exchanges.

(5)

A: What are the numbers [of unemployment] going to come down to?

B: As Sir Brian said, I think it's impossible to actually say . . .

(6)

A: When unemployment goes over 3 million, that adds to crime?

B: I think one has to be very careful in making that equation because it looks as though the criminals are to be found among the unemployed, and this simply isn't true.

(7)

A: What could the prime minister do about it?

B: Ah, that's really for him to answer, not for me, I think.

In both responses, B either states openly, as in (5), or implies, as in (6), that the question posed is in some way flawed. The answer to the question is impossible. A variation of this subtype is to declare the question wrongly addressed. The speaker in (7) presents himself as one who should not be asked the question because of his status or position. On the other hand, the refusal to answer the question posed may be voiced explicitly, as in the case of B's opt-out in (2) above. As I have argued elsewhere (Galasiński, 1996a), all such exchanges have one main common feature. The speaker's evasion is overt; the speaker more or less directly signals that he or she is not going to be cooperative. Deceptive communication, however, is clandestine. To succeed, the speaker must conceal her or his deceptive goals. Overt evasion, therefore, cannot be deceptive. To evade overtly means to give up the possibility of deceptiveness of the evasive utterance.

There are, however, cases in which the speaker not only evades the question but also tries not to make it manifest to the questioner. In acts of covert evasion, the speaker attempts to conceal that he or she does not give a cooperative answer. The response is meant by the speaker to pretend that it answers the question, whereas in fact it does not. A similar category—*sleight-of-hand*—was introduced by Sluzki, Beavin, Tarnopolsky, and Veron (1967; cf. also Bavelas et al., 1990a). The category, however, was developed more as a means of describing how answers appeared to be cooperative. It seems that the approach is complementary to that advocated here.

Semantically, questions can be thought of as incomplete propositions (cf. Harris, 1991). The questioner through his or her question seeks some information. The information sought, the proposition that answers the question is its focus (see Graesser & Franklin, 1990; Kreuz & Graesser, 1993). Thus, if someone asks, "Why did you leave so early?" the focus of the question consists of a proposition stating the reasons for the addressee's leaving (so) early. The addressee, in turn, can be thought of relative to the focal argument of the focus proposition, that is, *what* or *who* is referred to in the proposition, as opposed to *how* they are referred to. The reasons are the focus of the question, but it is the addressee who is focused on. The focus of the question may also be just an argument of a proposition. Thus, if the question is, say, "Who's drunk the milk?" the focus is the person who did it.

The typology of acts of covert evasion that is offered below is based on the semantics of questions and answers. It follows Wilson's (1990) postulates for a more formally based study of evasion. I shall argue that a speaker trying to evade the question covertly gives an answer that manipulates the semantic content of the question. The answerer, although pretending to answer the question, in fact, answers a different one. In other words, the speaker manipulates the focus of the question.

Let me assume that X is the focus of a question. I propose that there are three main types of acts of covert evasion. First, the speaker can refer to X within the textual context not focused on by the question. That is, X becomes an argument in a proposition that is not focal to the question. Second, the speaker can refer to Y as the focus of the question and refer to Y in the textual context laid out by the question. The answer involves a proposition that is demanded by the question, yet the focal argument is changed. Third, Y can be offered as the question's focus; moreover, the speaker can do it within a different textual context from the one demanded by the question. Thus, the speaker does not provide a response that can be regarded as focal to the question. Let me clarify the above using an example:

(8)

A: Did you welcome in that case the vigorous contribution to the debate made by Lady Thatcher? Were you pleased that she organized it this way?

B: Lady Thatcher is a remarkable political figure. She's done a great deal for this country. She has very strong views. She is still a member of Parliament in the House of Lords. She is entitled to express her views. She has done, she is doing, and she will continue to do so.

A asks two questions, thereby giving B some choice as to which question to answer. In both questions, A seeks to know something about the addressee; it is *you* that determines the focal proposition of the question. It is also the argument of which such attributes as *being pleased* (or similar) should be predicated. B, a British prime minister, presents "Lady Thatcher" as the argument of the focus proposition, however, in his stead. Moreover, he uses attributes that are not focused on in the question to describe the argument.

Changing the Textual Context of the Question

The first of the types of covert evasion consists in the speaker/answerer's reference to the focus (or the argument in the focus proposition) in terms different from those demanded by the questioner. The speaker may choose a number of options within the category. The answerer may speak of the issue in question yet say things that are not warranted by the question's content. The speaker can also reformulate the question's demand. While maintaining a close relationship between the question and the answer, that is, pretending to satisfy the question's focus, the speaker answers a different question. Finally, the answerer may broaden the scope of the answer. Thus, although the questioner asks a more or less specific question, the answerer puts the focus within a more general context.

Witness the following examples in which the textual context of the focus of the question is changed.

(9)

A: What will the KPN [Confederation of Independent Poland] exactly do, if it takes over power tomorrow?

B: If we take over power, first of all, people will have some prospect that within weeks—weeks, not years—the economic situation will start to improve. [*translated from Polish*]

(10)

A: . . . Would it be a blessing if the Danes voted no?

B: Well, we have to see how they vote. They've surprised us before, but I would have thought the odds are probably for voting yes. But we've made it very clear, there's no question of bullying them; if they say no, that decision will have to be accepted.

In both cases, B refers to the same event as the questioner does: takeover of power and the Danish vote (respectively). In both cases, however, the response does not provide the questioner with the answer that the questioner demanded. I think it is particularly this type of evasion that shows well that covert evasion is about pretending to answer cooperatively. The speaker does take up the object of the question, maintaining in such a way a cohesive link with it. The answer, however, is irrelevant.

On the other hand, (11) and (12) below are cases of reformulating the demand of the question. The questioner provides the answerer with such a possibility by focusing the question on the answerer. In such a way, while pretending to satisfy the question's demand by focusing the answer on him- or herself, the speaker provides an answer that is irrelevant.

(11)

A: Do you want a tougher regime in these secure places?

B: I want a regime that helps them [inmates] face up to their responsibility, to go and behave in a more mature and more sociable way in a community.

(12)

A: Do you defend the right of the tobacco industry to urge the pupils in Elaine Foster's school to smoke something which will damage their health?

B: I defend the right of the tobacco industry to advertise their product.

In both exchanges, B does refer to the question posed; in (11), B speaks of what he wants, and, in the case of (12), B says what she defends. The form of the responses is similar to the focus proposition projected by the question. Nonetheless, in both cases, B evades the yes or no answer, formulating the answer to suit his or her needs.

Finally, exchanges in (13) and (14) below are instances in which, although keeping the relationship with the question, the speaker broadens the scope of the utterance.

(13)

A: As a practical matter, Mr. President, do you agree with the governor when he says that the middle class—do your numbers agree that the taxes on the middle class have gone up?

B: I think that everybody's paying too much taxes. . . .

(14)

A: How has the national debt personally affected each of you . . .?

B: I think that the national debt affected everybody . . .

In (13), the question referred only to taxes on the middle class. The answerer, however, refers to taxes in general—enlarging the scope of the answer. A similar strategy can be observed in (14). The answerer does speak of the national debt— as the question demands—yet he speaks of the national debt affecting everyone, not just himself. Although speaker B in (14) gives an answer that is not demanded by the questioner, that is, he does not focus on the ways the national debt affected him, I still view his answer as maintaining the focus of the question. First, the exchange is part of a larger section of the debate devoted to the national debt; in other words, the debt has been the focus of a number of question-answer exchanges. Second, it seems to me that the speaker attempts to maintain a cohesive link between his answer and the question. He tries to talk about the same thing as the questioner asks, attempting thereby not only to evade the question but also to mask it.

Changing the Focus of the Question

The second type of covert evasion involves the speaker's changing the focus (or the focal argument) of the question. It is put, however, within the context demanded by the question. In other words, the argument, which is changed, is talked about within the textual context demanded by the question. For example,

(15)

A: Do you think we have a duty to do that—not just peacekeeping but also peace-making?

B: I think that UN generally is gonna have to move from peacekeeping to peace-making. I think that's a fact of life.

(16)

A: Do you regard it as essential to your survival as the leader [of the Labour Party] to win the next general election?

B: Well, I think it's essential for the Labour Party and it's essential for this country that we win the next election. . . .

The answerer makes at least two changes with regard to the focus of the question in (15). First, the question asks about a duty, whereas the answerer changes it to mere necessity ("having to"), disposing of the moral aspect of the issue. Second, and more important, the main object of the question, "we" (understood, more or less, as Britain), is changed into the UN. The UN is referred to as the focal argument of the question. Similarly, in (16), B substitutes the Labour Party for himself. In both cases, B replies using the form of the focus proposition demanded by the question, thereby masking evasion.

Changing the Focus and the Textual Context of the Question

The last type of utterances evading questions covertly consists in changing both the argument and the context within which it is referred to. Once again, there are a number of ways in which the speaker can engage in this strategy. The speaker can issue an utterance that includes a proposition that is not coherently related to the question. The relationship between the question and the answer, and the pragmatic relevance of the latter, is based on operating within the same general knowledge frame (for a detailed analysis of knowledge structures and their relationship to discourse understanding, see, e.g., Brown & Yule, 1983), pretending thereby that it actually is a cooperative response (cf. van der Meij, 1987). Another option is to choose one of the elements the question refers to and respond by focusing on it. Finally, the speaker may address a proposition presupposed by the question. The speaker in such a way covertly puts the question in a different perspective. Witness the following examples.

(17)

A: But you don't say that you don't welcome her [Lady Thatcher's] involvement in the debate like that?

B: We have perhaps the freest, most open democracy in the world. You can't close that democracy down.

(18)

A: Can you keep that [level of inflation] for the lifetime of this Parliament?

B: Well, the depreciation of sterling may have a once-for-all impact on prices. We have very little room for maneuver on the target that we have set ourselves.

In the case of (17), B may count on A's appreciation that freedom to say whatever one wants is an essential part of a democratic political system. On that basis, B's response, although evasive, can be viewed as operating within the same knowledge frame and thus be pragmatically relevant to the question. Similarly, inflation has a lot to do with currency exchange rates, price levels, and so forth—

this is the background knowledge drawn on in B's answer in (18). In neither case, however, is the question answered.

Exchanges in (19) and (20) are examples of the answerers choosing another focus for their utterance.

(19)

A: Isn't there the case for taking the prime minister out of the center of the whole thing [honors system]? Why should, for instance, he or a prime minister be able to reward newspaper editors who backed his or her party in general elections?

B: Well, the issue, it seems to me, the people are going to have the opportunity to nominate in a much more open way. One of the things which hasn't been mentioned about the statement today is that for the first time, there will be a nomination form.

(20)

A: They tell me that you've risen in the betting to be the next chancellor of the Exchequer.

B: We've got an excellent chancellor of the Exchequer, very unfairly criticized. He's been laying foundations for the prospect, the exciting prospect I've been talking about.

In (19)—just as A—B, a cabinet minister, also refers to the honors system yet focuses on an aspect that is irrelevant in view of the question. A asks two questions about the prime minister, whereas B responds with a statement about nominations for honors. On the other hand, (20)—already mentioned in excerpt (4)— is even more interesting. The question is about B and his chances to become the chancellor of the Exchequer—the one in office being relatively irrelevant (at least insofar as his "popularity" is concerned). A's question refers to the post, not the person, as B attempts to reformulate. Note also a buildup of cohesion within B's utterance. Each clause is closely linked to the previous one, giving appearances of relevance. Moreover, B ends with a metaproposition about previous discourse that is probably, yet again, intended to suggest the utterance's relevance.

Finally, in (21), while remaining in the same knowledge frame, the answerer reformulates the questioner's demands.

(21)

A: What do you think should be the response to the BMA's [British Medical Association] warning that the sick people are being turned away due to cash shortages before the end of the financial year?

B: Well, the irony is that BMA said it today, and only yesterday the Labour spokesman said, there's being a great cash bonanza in the NHS, and indeed he was beginning to see that there were arguments in favor of NHS trusts.

B's response is intended to, as it were, give a new reading to A's question. A's question presupposes that there are cash shortages within the NHS. B, a secretary of state, defies that proposition, however, by bringing the claim of her opposition counterpart. In such a way, she not only does not answer the question but also challenges its content.

DECEPTIVENESS OF EVASION

Having mapped out the types of evasive actions, I would now like to address the problem posed in the title of this chapter: deceptiveness of evasion. In the following discussion, I shall answer two questions. First, are all acts of evasion inherently deceptive? As I pointed out at the beginning of this chapter, an affirmative answer to this question is a prevalent assumption in the literature on deceptive communication. Because I shall answer the question negatively, the second question will be whether evasion can be thought of as deception at all, and if yes, how.

The very nature of deceptive communication is that it is clandestine. Speakers/deceivers cannot reveal their intentions to deceive without running the risk of failing in the deceptive attempts. This, together with the consideration that evasion can be overt, is sufficient to support the argument that evasive communication does not have to be deceptive. Speakers can more or less openly inform the questioners that they will not answer the questions posed.

Opting out, one of the Gricean ways of not observing the cooperative principle, is probably the most overt way of evading the question. The speaker can simply say that he or she will not cooperate. In (2), the speaker said,

(2)

B: I refuse to make this kind of judgements. [*translated from Polish*]

and plainly informed that he was not going to answer the question and thus evaded the question posed for him. All responses such as "no comment" or "nothing further to add" do the same thing. They are an overt way of not answering the question.

Consider also (22) and (23), examples given in Dillon (1990, pp. 154-155).

(22)

A: How old are you?

B: Don't worry, they'll let me into the bar.

(23)

A: How old are you?

B: Oh no, I left my headlights on.

Let us assume that in both cases, A does want to know B's age. In (22), B does not answer a specific question asked by A, giving only (depending on the context, of course) a more or less obvious indication of her or his age. B's response triggers an implicature that includes both the indication of age and an indication of the reluctance to be more specific. Also, in this example, evasiveness is clear to A, and this, in turn, means that deception is out of the question. (23) differs in that it offers only an indication of B's unwillingness to cooperate. The situation does not change significantly even if B's utterance in (23) is false, and B is lying to A. One can still hardly speak of deception because truth or falsity of that utterance is simply irrelevant (cf. Ng & Bradac, 1993). Moreover, B does not even have to intend A to believe her or his utterance.

Now, can evasion be deceptive at all? The intuitive answer to that question is affirmative. Witness the exchange in (24).

(24)

A: Would you vote for the Senate antiabortion bill?

B: What kind of stance can a member of a Christian party take? [*translated from Polish*]

B responds to A's question using an implicature. The inferential process is something such as this: Christian parties are against abortion; a member of a Christian party would therefore vote for an antiabortion bill; B is a member of a Christian party; therefore B would vote for the Senate antiabortion bill. A is bound to assume that B wanted to implicate an affirmative answer, and, indeed, B's response may well be one that means "Quite obviously, what a dumb question!" Should B not mean it, however, A may be deceived. If, for some reason, B does not want to say that he would not vote for the bill, he opted for a devious message, one in which the speaker does not commit to the proposition she or he implies (cf. Bowers et al., 1977). Clearly, B's response in (24) can be deceptive. Moreover, it is also evasive. The conclusion that might follow is that evasion can be deceptive.

I do not think, however, that this is the sort of answer one is looking for. Evasion is not a type of speech act; it cannot be analyzed in the same way as statements, requests, orders, promises, and other acts. Declarations, warnings, or confessions can easily be used by an evasive speaker. Furthermore, the problem of evasion arises only on the level of a *response* to a question, that is, at least on the level of question-answer exchange—a structure going beyond a single utterance/ speech act or its type. Thus, one can speak of an evasive speech act (in a particular context), rather than a speech act of evasion (for a more detailed discussion of this point, see Chapter 7). Indeed, B's remark in (24) is not inherently evasive. It is easy to imagine it as part of a speech. For example,

(25)

B: At all the meetings I have attended, people raise the issue of abortion. People ask whether I would vote for the Senate antiabortion bill. I don't like answering such questions. I think it is insulting. *What kind of stance can a member of a Christian party take?* [*contrived*]

Embedded in such an utterance, (24) is not evasive. Because there is no question, the situation of evasion does not arise. For one reason or another, however, the speaker may want to imply his or her intentions to vote for an antiabortion bill, despite the actual ones to the contrary, and thus commit an act of deception.

Is evasion not deceptive, then? It is—but in a different manner. First of all, let me come back to the basic distinction between overt and covert evasion. In the case of the former, the speaker signals to the addressee that he or she will for some reason not cooperate in answering the question (for a further discussion, see Galasiński, 1996a). In the latter case, the speaker does not do it—he or she simply does not cooperate. Intuitively then, covert evasion is an example of a violation of conversation maxims (cf. Grice, 1975) and seems to be a perfect candidate for being deceptive.

Let us then consider again the exchange in (8).

(8)

A: Did you welcome in that case the vigorous contribution to the debate made by Lady Thatcher? Were you pleased that she organized it this way?

B: Lady Thatcher is a remarkable political figure. She's done a great deal for this country. She has very strong views. She is still a member of Parliament in the House of Lords. She is entitled to express her views. She has done, she is doing, and she will continue to do so.

Can B's response be regarded as deceptive? Not if we are looking at the level of the statement only. B may well have said something true, and thus there is nothing deceptive about it.

According to Grice (1981), language users generally assume that communicators will not violate conversational procedures. People will normally be truthful, relevant, and clear; they will not say too much or too little. Evasion is a violation of this assumption. In the case of (8), and indeed that of covert evasion in general, the speaker produces an utterance that is meant to pretend that it is relevant, whereas in fact it is not. An evader then deceives the addressee insofar as the evader wants the addressee to believe something false about the very utterance the speaker produced as a response to the question. Deceptiveness of evasion, therefore, is *metadiscursive*.

Evasion should be described as the speaker's attempt to control the flow of discourse. In overt evasion, the speaker questions the warrantability of previous discourse. Refusing to answer a question, or even answering it indirectly without a full commitment by the speaker, challenges the questioner's right to ask it. But the speaker can also do it by a clandestine violation of the Gricean maxim of relevance. In this case, the addressee is a target of a manipulative action: The addressee is intended to accept the relevance of an irrelevant answer without being aware of it. Furthermore, the speaker, manipulating the focus of the question, answers a question different from the one asked, making sure thereby that he or she has control over how the exchange develops. In such a way, evasion performs its controlling function.

It is not necessarily the questioner, however, who is the target of the manipulation, especially in the domain of public speaking. In the case of interviews, for example, there is also a third party who is the hearer—the public. Even if the interviewer realizes that her or his question is being evaded, the public may not.

CONCLUDING REMARKS

The main objective of this chapter was to examine a commonly made assumption as to the inherent deceptiveness of evasion. To examine this problem, I first dealt with the conceptual problem: I argued that the existing definitions of evasion do not stand the test of data. I submitted that evasive communicative action should be defined using semantic irrelevance. I then argued that only covert evasion, one in which the speaker pretends to provide a cooperative answer, can be considered as deceptiveness. Furthermore, I argued that one cannot view the deceptiveness of an evasive speech act as necessarily a case of the deceptiveness of evasion. In other words, it is not the falsity of a statement used by the speaker to evade the question that constitutes deceptiveness of an evasive act. Evasion is deceptive in that it constitutes an attempt to induce in the addressee a false belief as to the relevance of the answer. An evasive speaker, therefore, deceives the addressee insofar as her or his own utterance is concerned. Deceptiveness of evasion, therefore, is metadiscursive deception. The next chapter will consider the notion of metadiscursive deception in more detail.

5

Metadiscursive Deception

In the previous chapter, I have argued that deceptiveness of evasion cannot be likened to that of a statement falsely representing reality. Although the aim of a liar is to say something false about an extralinguistic state of affairs, the aim of the evasive speaker is to render a response relevant to the question the speaker is answering. Deceptiveness of covert evasion is metadiscursive; it is aimed at falsely representing the very utterance that is evasive. What follows from this argument is that deceptive strategies can be categorized into two main clusters with reference to the object of misrepresentation. There are strategies in which extralinguistic reality is misrepresented and, on the other hand, those whose object is the utterance of which they are part. The latter strategies, like evasion, are what I have called metadiscursive deception. They are attempts of the speaker/deceiver to make the addressee believe that the utterance the speaker is issuing is cooperative, whereas in fact it is not. In this chapter, I shall explore metadiscursive deception.

STRATEGIES OF METADISCURSIVE DECEPTION

In the previous chapter, I discussed the notion of conversational demand introduced by Dascal (1977) and Holdcroft (1987). The two linguists propose that an utterance is relevant to some other utterance if the former meets the conversational demand of the latter. Conversational demand, in turn, is defined by Holdcroft as an illocutionary act whose determinants are its illocutionary force (that of promising, ordering, or thanking, for example) and its propositional content (what is promised, ordered, or thanked for). It can also be extended to some higher aim in discourse. Satisfying the conversational demand is the core of the utterance's cooperativeness. Thus, apart from satisfying the precondition of relevance, the utterance must also satisfy conditions of clarity, truthfulness, and informativeness. As is the case with conversational demand, cooperation in general can be satisfied by the function of the utterance as well as its propositional content. To answer a question, the speaker may have to issue a statement (i.e., an utterance with a certain function) with its propositional content satisfying the focus of the question. Furthermore, the proposition carried by the content of the utterance is normally expected to be an accurate rendition of the state of affairs (maxim of truthfulness satisfied by the propositional content). An apology is normally expected to refer to a wrong deed of the speaker (relevance satisfied by the propositional content). The relevance of a weatherperson, on the other hand, will normally be satisfied by issuing an utterance with the function of a forecast.

Metadiscursive deception is an attempt to render a noncooperative utterance as cooperative. Because noncooperation can relate either to the function of the utterance or to its propositional content, there are two main types of metadiscursive deception. The speaker may attempt to misrepresent the actual function of the utterance or its propositional content. Although the distinction offered here comprehensively describes metadiscursive deception, the strategies I shall discuss, however, are unlikely to cover all possibilities. I intend here to offer a conceptual framework of the phenomenon, illustrated by a number of examples, rather than a review of all the strategies of metadiscursive deception.

I shall describe the metadiscursive strategies of deception in reference to masking. I shall follow Ng and Bradac (1993) in arguing that as masks, the strategies make reality appear different from what it actually is. The two researchers are, however, interested in different types of masks from the ones described here. Ng and Bradac focus on the way lexico-grammatical resources of language can be used to represent extralinguistic reality. I am interested in how certain linguistic means are used to render the very utterance of which they are part. Masks described by Ng and Bradac show true information in a partial or incomplete way, and thus they do not withhold information. The masks I shall be discussing, on the other hand, are aimed at rendering an uncooperative utterance cooperative. They are not, therefore, aimed at presenting reality in a partial way; rather, they are aimed at making the discourse seem different from what it is. They are aimed at falsifying a state of affairs; in this particular case, the utterances are part of and thus are a strategy of deception.

As I signaled above, I shall be discussing two main types of metadiscursive strategies: those misrepresenting the functions of the utterance and those misrepresenting its contents. Within the former category, I shall discuss two strategies: concealing evasion and concealing a direct attack (a rhetorical mood expressly forbidden by the rules of the debate; see below). The latter category will include implicit misrepresentation and manipulation of felicity conditions of speech acts.

Although I have defined evasion by the semantic relationship between the propositional contents of the answer and the question, I still propose that concealing it is a mask of the function of the utterance, rather than its propositional content. The reason for this differentiation is that although covert evasion is intended to be semantically irrelevant, its deceptiveness consists in getting the addressee (the questioner) to believe that the utterance performs the function of answering the question. As such, it seemingly contributes to furthering the overall goal of the unfolding exchange. The evader wants to misrepresent her or his utterance's function within a larger stretch of discourse.

Masking Uncooperative Functions

Concealing Evasion

The first set of strategies I shall discuss here in some detail are related to evasion. I shall be interested in the speaker's attempts to conceal his or her evasion of a question. The main task of the evader is to construct the utterance in such a way that it looks as if it satisfies the conversational demands of the question. Because I described the strategies of concealing evasion in detail elsewhere (see Galasiński, 1996b), I shall limit the discussion here to a few examples.
Consider now the following exchanges.

(1)

A: Where do you stand on gun control, and what do you plan to do about it?

B: I support the right to keep and bear arms. . . . I believe we have to have is some way of checking handguns before they're sold, to check the criminal history, the mental health of people who're buying them. . . .

(2)

A: Is there any tangible evidence that there will be a change in the Chinese position? Can you see any softening of it at all?

B: I can see the prospect of getting back into a dialogue with China. I think that is the only sensible way forward. . . .

(3)

A: Did you welcome in that case the vigorous contribution to the debate made by Lady Thatcher? Were you pleased that she organized it this way?

B: Lady Thatcher is a remarkable political figure. She's done a great deal for this country. She has very strong views. She is still a member of Parliament in the House of Lords. She is entitled to express her views. She has done, she is doing, and she will continue to do so.

The three examples above show the concealment of the noncooperation by employing a number of semantic means: thematic position of the focal argument, parallel syntactic forms, and "tight" cohesion (see Galasiński, 1996b). In the first exchange, A demands an answer in which B, a U.S. presidential candidate, should focus on his views on gun control and actions he plans to take to (or not to) enforce stricter regulations in gun purchasing. B does exactly what is, technically, demanded by the question–he focuses on himself. He puts self-reference in the theme of the sentence. He himself, therefore, becomes what the sentence tells us, its starting point (e.g., Halliday, 1994; Halliday & Hasan, 1985). There is no doubt that his answer will actually relate to his "manifesto" on gun control. Yet the answer is far too general to count as a cooperative one.

In exchange (2), on the other hand, a senior Tory politician, who is unlikely to want to comment directly on the toughness of the Chinese regime, evades the question and makes a prediction about future relations with China. Still, he chooses to reflect the syntactic form of the question: "Can you see" becomes "I can see." A different device is used in (3). After putting the main argument of the question's focus in the thematic position, the speaker, a prime minister unlikely to want to directly criticize a former prime minister, repeats the form of the first clause in the next six. Parallelism of the form is a way to suggest that there is a connection between sentences (Cook, 1989). Furthermore, repeating the message (in a different form) may also suggest that the speaker is actually answering the question. Admittedly, one would not normally repeat irrelevant things, especially if one wanted to hide them.

There are also pragmatic ways of concealing evasion. The speaker may indicate a willingness and/or readiness to answer the question. It seems plausible to assume that in such a situation, the speaker will be understood as implying that his or her response will be cooperative. The speaker may employ four strategies here: explicit or implicit indication of readiness, licenses of uncooperativeness, and hedging. Licences of uncooperativeness and hedging are different from the first two strategies in that indications of the speaker's willingness can only be inferred. In both cases, the speaker wants to give an impression that should the answer appear to be uncooperative, it is not her or his intention.

Consider now the following exchanges.

(4)

    A: Will you make a pledge tonight below which an income level that you will not go below? I am looking for numbers, not just the concept.

    B: I can tell you this. I will not raise taxes on the middle class to pay for these programs.

(5)

A: Where do you stand on gun control, and what do you plan to do about it?

B: I think you put your finger on a major problem. I talk about strengthening the American family, and it's very difficult to strengthen the family if people are scared to walk down to the corner store and, you know, send their kids down to get a loaf of bread. It's very hard. I have been fighting for a very strong anticrime legislation. . . .

(6)

A1: How has the national debt personally affected each of you?

B1: I think the national debt affects everybody. Obviously, it has a lot to do with interest rates. . . .

A2: How has it affected you . . . personally?

B2: ⌈I am sure it has. I love my grandchildren. I wanna think that—

A3: ⌊How has it affected you personally?

B3: I want to think that they're gonna be able to afford an education. I think that that's an important part of being a parent. If the question, if you're, maybe I won't get it wrong, are you suggesting that if somebody has means, then the national debt doesn't affect them? Help me with the question, and I'll try to answer it.

In exchange (4), the speaker, a U.S. presidential candidate, overtly indicates his readiness to answer the question. In exchange (5), with another candidate, the comment on the importance of the issue serves that particular function. Arguably, if someone signals that an important problem is touched on in the question, it is only natural to expect that some attention will be devoted to it. In exchange (6), with the same candidate as in (5), B's third move is interesting here. Not being able to answer the question and being pressed by the questioner (a member of the audience), B changes his strategy and starts speculating about the question posed. He analyzes what the questioner meant. To get his answer right, B must interpret the question correctly in the first place. By doing this, B implicitly suggests that he is ready to answer. The strategy is reinforced by B's overt request to the questioner to help him understand the question.

Finally, in (7) below, the answerer licenses his problems with answering the questions by indicating that he does not have the benefit of fortune-telling. In such a way, I argue, he pretends to be willing to answer the question. He is hindered, but he is not uncooperative. Ancillary to his strategy seems B's attempt at positive self-presentation—presumably calculated to counter any possible damage made by recalling the problematic aspects of B's past but also indicating that he has little to fear from the question and thus he is not dodging it. B also attempts to undermine somewhat the validity of questions concerning the past and thus makes answering the question posed for him at least problematic. Witness:

(7)

A: If you had to do it over again, would you put on the nation's uniform, and, if elected, could you in good conscience send someone to war?

B: If I had to do it over again, I might answer your question better. You know, I've been in public life a long time, and no one had ever questioned my role, and I was asked a lot of questions about things that happened a long time ago, and I don't think I answered them as well as I could have. . . .

Concealing Attack

Another example of metadiscursive masking strategies comes from Polish presidential debates. I have argued elsewhere (Galasiński, 1998) that the debaters used mitigating devices as a means of manipulating the flow of the speaker's discourse and, furthermore, as a clandestine means to license an attack on the other speaker. In such a way, mitigating devices are part of the strategy of metadiscursive deception.

Aleksander Kwaśniewski and Lech Wałęsa were the two candidates for the presidency of Poland in the second round of the elections on November 19, 1995. Two television debates between the two candidates were held in the week preceding the election. According to the moderator, the Polish television tried to persuade the candidates to face each other directly during the debates. Neither of the election camps agreed to that, however. Thus, at the beginning of each debate, the moderator explained that the candidates were not to address each other but only to answer questions coming from either the moderator or the journalists invited by the candidates. Each candidate was represented by two journalists.

Politicians use the debate as a means of gaining advantage over their opponent (Benoit & Wells, 1996). Forfeiting the right to speak directly to each other meant a severe reduction in the candidates' ability both to attack one another's positions and, even more acutely, to defend against potential attacks. In answering questions, both candidates could speak *of* each other and in such a way attack, that is, attempt to damage the image of the other candidate (Benoit & Wells, 1996). Their ability to defend themselves, that is, to repair their potentially damaged image, however, was significantly reduced, because the moderator or the journalists may not have asked a question that would have allowed them to do so.

As might have been expected, in both debates the candidates often broke the rule of no direct address. They addressed the other candidate directly, for example, by asking a question or challenging a point. Or they directly responded to the opponent's statement, although the response was irrelevant to the question that had already been asked. But violations of the rules by the two politicians could damage their image. The speakers therefore implemented a number of strategies to mitigate the violations.

Mitigating devices are all those expressions that are used to soften the intention behind the unwelcome action (Ng & Bradac, 1993; see also Brown & Levinson, 1987). Both candidates attempted to present their violations as in some way justified and thus less reprehensible, less deserving of the social sanction. Furthermore, the mitigation devices also licensed more general uncooperativeness (cf. Mura, 1983). Three main strategies were used by the speakers: describing the rule violation as insignificant, excusing oneself as under pressure to issue the violating utterance, and reasserting one's unwillingness to breach the rules.

The two politicians' discursive actions described above are not only aimed at licensing violations of the debate's rules, or merely some redressive actions aimed at preserving the positive face (Brown & Levinson, 1987) of the moderator or, perhaps, the journalists. Using the mitigating devices allows the two politicians to pretend to communicate in accordance with the rules of the debate and thus pretend to cooperate by abiding by the agreed-on rules. The mitigating devices also enable the speakers to manipulate the content and direction of the debate. In such a way, (the pretense of) cooperation operates here on two levels. Locally, it refers to the requirement that the politicians abide by the rules of the debate, as imposed on them by the moderator, and which go beyond the "normal" communicative practice. More globally, (the pretense of) cooperation operates also on the level of the Gricean cooperative principle (Grice, 1975). In this sense, politicians pretend to produce cooperative contributions to the debate that are relevant, clear, and truthful and that contain the right amount of information. In other words, the Gricean cooperative principle, while maintaining its global validity, is also appropriated by the local context and the activity type in which the communicators are engaged (cf. Sarangi & Slembrouck, 1992).

Of particular interest about the politicians' rule-breaking actions is that they appear to be used predominantly for the purpose of defense: The speaker has been attacked, and he is compelled to repair the damaged image. And yet, as I shall show below, every defensive action is always followed by an attack. The defense therefore is hardly what it seems; it is a way of getting away with a direct attack. Defense is used as a means of mitigating the attack. Consider the following example.

(8)

English translation of Wałęsa's turn:

507-511:   My counterpartner talks of some confrontation, so he is preparing NATO for a war with whom? With Lithuania, probably, because Russia has good relations with America and NATO, too, so we shall be arming and joining NATO because we shall wage war on Lithuania? Absurd. There is no other way at the moment.

512: K: Who said it?

513: W: But, well, but when one says such things, this is what it looks like. . . .

514: K: This is what you understood of it. . . .

English translation of Kwaśniewski's turn:

529-531: K: Very briefly, I shall start with this Lithuania, though. I want to say clearly not for a moment have I thought [or] think, and it does not follow from the words I said here, that our entry to NATO should be a confrontation with whoever.

532-534:   I have said on numerous occasions that it is to be an element of stability and not confrontation. If anyone understands me differently, they either are ill-willed or simply don't want to understand.

Wałęsa starts his attack (not breaking the agreed rules of the debate) by imputing to his opponent that he was talking about confrontation with Lithuania and declares the stance to be absurd (lines 507-511). Kwaśniewski challenges the point, interjecting into Wałęsa's utterance (line 512), yet the latter does not withdraw his claim. Later on, therefore, Kwaśniewski launches his defense, mitigating the move by presenting it as brief and by the use of *jednak* ("however," "though"), acknowledging his willingness to answer the question posed for him (lines 529-531). He does not merely attempt to repair the potential damage to his image caused by Wałęsa, however; he also attacks Wałęsa's integrity by accusing him of ill will.

Now, as signaled above, both politicians consistently use mitigators to introduce a defensive move and not an attack. It is the defense that is constructed as the reason for the potential uncooperativeness. Defense is used as a "justifiable means" of launching an attack on the opponent. Although a direct attack can hardly be mitigated as justifiable given the rules of the debate, a direct defense can. The politicians use the mitigation-defense-attack pattern because only such a pattern is capable of potentially safeguarding them against a possible boomerang effect in public opinion.

More generally, the two politicians violate the public's expectations of their behavior in the debates on two counts. First, by attempting to pass off the instances of uncooperative behavior as permissible, both speakers are using those seemingly insignificant fragments of their discourse to achieve one of the most important goals of the debate—to preserve their positive image and to reduce that of their opponent's. Not only do the mitigators license the brief irrelevancies—"remarks" or "sentences," as the speakers portray them—in the answers, they license the opportunities to address the opponent and, even more important, to attack the opponent directly.

Moreover, by licensing the immediate irrelevance of the offending utterances, mitigating devices are also used to mask their actual function. While pretending that they heed the need to be cooperative, the two speakers mask their uncooperativeness. Both speakers have a hidden goal in their communicative actions (see Castelfranchi & Poggi, 1994). This hidden goal is to prevent the audience (both in the studio and the television viewers) from inferring that the point of using mitigating devices goes beyond merely acknowledging the local uncooperativeness. The real objective is to prepare the ground for the coming attack. In such a way also, mitigating devices are metadiscursively deceptive.

Finally, focusing the mitigation on acknowledging the rules of the debate preserves the positive faces (see Brown & Levinson, 1987) of the moderator, the journalists, and the public at large. There were no attempts to direct the mitigation at the opponent. This enables the politicians to maintain the appearance of cooperativeness and politeness while derogating their opponent.

The attempts to preserve one's image and damage that of the opponent operate at two levels, then. Mitigators are aimed at licensing the opportunity first to defend and, more important, to attack the opponent. This is the level of licensing noncooperation on the global level of the cooperative principle. Locally, however, it is done precisely by the appearance of abiding by the rules of the debate and the concern for others' positive face. It is on this level that the speaker attempts to win the audience perceptions of him not only as a communicator of sorts but also as a participant in a social event. It is possible to argue, therefore, that the strategies of presenting oneself as talking under pressure or reluctantly breaking the rules of the debate are not accidental. Rather, they serve locally to create a certain perception of the politician of good will (see also Hamilton & Mineo, 1998).

Masking Uncooperative Contents

Metadiscursive deception concerns also the contents of utterances. There are two main strategies I shall discuss here. First, I shall examine the issue of deceptive implications, and I shall argue that contrary to their frequent conceptualizations in the literature as one of the types of the deceptive message, in fact they are a means of conveying misrepresentation. Second, in this view, I shall also discuss manipulation of felicity conditions.

Implicit Misrepresentations

As I argued in Chapter 3, implicit misrepresentations are no different from the strategies in which misrepresentation is carried in the explicit part of the utterance. Consider two more examples.

(9)

A: If we created one job a minute, it would still take 6 years to get everybody back to work. . . . And that's not a problem that is going to be solved by arguing about who is to blame for what. . . .

B: It's quite easy to just say, well, it will take 6 years for us to create that amount of jobs. It seems you're not doing much at the moment.

A: I was trying to indicate the scale of the problem.

(10)

A: Cigarettes are probably the most dangerous things circulating. . . . Not only would I push up taxes further on tobacco, I think I'd also consider very hard asking tobacco companies to make a contribution to NHS broadly equivalent to the acute burden they place on it.

B: I think it's essential to correct this notion that [A] was just propounding, that cigarette smokers are a burden on the society. We actually contribute about 30 million pounds a day in taxation, which I think would probably be more than running of the NHS.

Once again, misrepresentations in the two exchanges above are conveyed implicitly. In (9), B, using a conversational implicature, implies that A attempted to provide an excuse for his inability to act on the problems of employment. Maxims of quantity and, perhaps, relation (the utterance may be stating the obvious), are flouted. In (10), on the other hand, the misrepresentation is carried by a presupposition. B changes the one who actually places the burden on the NHS—in A's utterance, it is the cigarette companies; in B's, it is the smokers.

I think that the most plausible way in which to describe misrepresentation carried implicitly is as channels of deception, the means by which misrepresentations can be conveyed. Putting misrepresentation into the implicit part of the utterance is a means of concealing it and, at the same time, possibly enhancing its potential effectiveness. The misrepresentation may be particularly effective and, perhaps even more important, safe to make, if the utterance conveying it implicitly is itself true. The action that the deceiver is taking, therefore, is not using a distinct type of misrepresentation, but rather, the deceiver removes it to the background of her or his utterance or to what is implied by it. In such a way, the speaker masks the uncooperativeness of her or his utterance.

Particularly, presuppositions, whose manipulatory potential is well known (cf., e.g., Dillon, 1990; Harder & Kock, 1976), can be seen as a means of concealing the deceptive action. Presuppositions represent what is assumed in the utterance to be taken for granted. They are (or pretend to be) part of the background knowledge in the communicative situation and are unlikely to be challenged when used manipulatively (cf., e.g., Loftus, 1975). On the other hand, a misrepresentation that appears as a conversational implicature may be more visible than a presupposition, yet it is more difficult to challenge. The deceiver may simply deny the implication.

Felicity Conditions

The other way of conveying misrepresentation implicitly is related to the notion of felicity conditions of the utterance (speech act). Felicity conditions of speech acts are those conditions that have to obtain for a speech act to be appropriate (Austin, 1962; Searle, 1969). For example, for a promise to be felicitous, the speaker has to intend to fulfill his or her commitment; for an order to be felicitous, the ordered action must be "performable" (see Searle, 1969). Similarly to presuppositions, felicity conditions can be presented as a set of propositions whose truth is normally assumed by the participants in the communicative situation when a particular speech act is performed.

Consider now the following exchanges.

(11)

A: What does the panel think of John Major's decision [to sue for libel]? What does it say about Norman Lamont's handling and financing of his possession action that John Major is prepared to pay all his legal costs?

B: I think you are right. I think that the finger is pointed back at Norman Lamont.

(12)

A: Do the committed Europeans on the panel feel disappointment with the terrible events in the former Yugoslavia?

B: I am not sure that I really accept the connection between whether or not one is a committed European, and I think I would regard myself as such, and the disappointment which one feels not so much because Europe hasn't been able to solve this problem. . . .

In both cases, speakers B misrepresent what has been said in the questions. In (11), B ascribes the accusatory power to the questioner; in (12), B attributes to A a statement of the connection between being a committed European and feeling disappointment. (Admittedly, the questioner might have wanted the committed Europeans to answer the question, even if it may be seen as implying some sarcasm.) Also, in this case, the question gets represented as a claim. Both misrepresentations are constructed as agreements. The problem, however, is that B cannot felicitously agree with A in either of the cases. One of the felicity conditions of agreeing is that the statement one wants to agree with has to contain the same claim as the one the speaker who agrees wants to make. Yet in both exchanges, B misrepresents what was said. Moreover, B is in no position to agree with the questions.

It seems that there are two aspects of the misrepresentations of this type. First, there is no difference between them and the cases discussed with regard to implicit misrepresentations. Framing her or his utterance as an agreement, the speaker presupposes that what she or he agrees with has actually been said and that it is true, precisely by virtue of being put in the presupposition. Second, however, also at stake are the felicity conditions. Speakers B in (11) and (12) falsely presuppose that the conditions of the speech act of agreement obtain. Misrepresented, therefore, is the utterance pretending to be an agreement. (See also an analysis of the manipulation of the felicity conditions of apologies and denials in Giora, 1994.)

A false implication is an attempt to get the addressee to believe that the utterance or, more precisely, its propositional content, adheres to the assumption that speakers are normally cooperative. If a deceiver uses implicatures or presuppositions to conceal the act of misrepresentation, the concealment is also an act of deception. Deceptiveness of a false implication is metadiscursive. The argument is particularly strong in the case of manipulation of felicity conditions. A speaker's attempt to present his or her utterance as an agreement is precisely aimed at misrepresenting the utterance that is misrepresenting reality.

METADISCURSIVE DECEPTION

Metadiscursive strategies of deception are aimed at concealing the uncooperativeness of the utterance of which they are part. I have argued above that there are two main types of metadiscursive deception: strategies that intend to misrepresent the function of the utterance and those that attempt to show the propositional content of the utterance as cooperative. The four specific strategies of metadiscursive deception discussed above, however, do not exhaust the problem.

In this section, I would like to point to some other possibilities in mapping out the full range of metadiscursive strategies. Obfuscation seems to be one of the strategies that conceal the noncooperation on the level of communication itself. A speaker obfuscates when she or he intends the addressee not to understand the full import of the utterance. This can be done, for example, by the use of technical jargon, verbal cosmetics, or euphemisms (cf. Vincent & Castelfranchi, 1981). The speaker uses language merely to pretend to communicate. The speaker not only masks false or, indeed, true information but also attempts to deceive the target as to her or his communicative intentions. The strategy seems to be somewhat problematic for the dichotomy of strategies offered above. Still, I have decided not to introduce a new category, assuming communicativeness also to be a function, albeit, most basic, of utterances (see Nuyts, 1989).

The category of metadiscursive deception seems also to be useful in explaining deceptiveness of speech acts to which it is impossible to ascribe truth or falsity. Although neither true nor false, questions, promises, and commands can be deceptive, be it by presupposing something or by being insincere. The notorious "Have you stopped beating your wife?" is deceptive metadiscursively in that it conveys a false presupposition (assuming, of course, that the addressee has never beaten his wife). The question can hardly be thought of as an attempt to extract certain information from the addressee. Rather, it is used as a means to convey false information about the speaker. (On a different level, it may also be an attempt to get the addressee to admit to something he or she had never done; cf., e.g., Loftus, 1975; Shuy, 1993.) In such a way, it functions as a means of concealing the misrepresentation.

In the same way, someone knowingly promising something that he or she cannot do, thus violating one of the felicity conditions of promising, may well intend to present him- or herself as someone who indeed can do it. Giving an order, in turn, may be used to present oneself as someone in power to do it. Once again, although neither true nor false, such two utterances are a means of conveying a piece of information about the speaker implicitly. The category of metadiscursive deception provides a framework within which to analyze such acts. In such a way also, the analysis of lying proposed by Reboul (1994) is made problematic. Reboul significantly extends the definition of lying and proposes to analyze it as the violation of the sincerity condition, rather than the falsity or believed falsity of the prepositional content of the utterance. Apart from the significance of the believed falsity of the content of the utterance in distinguishing lies from insincere promises, the violation of a sincerity condition seems to be one of the most universal features of deception. There is no deception without the speaker being insincere. What Reboul seems to have achieved, therefore, is close to a definition of deception or, perhaps, manipulation in general, rather than a definition of lying. I shall return to the problem in the final chapter.

METADISCURSIVE DECEPTION AND
A THEORY OF DECEPTIVE COMMUNICATION

Metadiscursive deception is also a useful element in the incorporation of the linguistic element into an overall theory of deception. Such a theory—described by the author as the first comprehensive attempt at a theory of deception—was proposed by Whaley (1982) on the basis of military deception. In what follows, I shall attempt to discuss linguistic deception in its terms.

Whaley (1982) proposes that deception is the distortion of perceived reality that operationally is done by changing the pattern of distinguishing characteristics. The deceiver's task is to profess the false in the face of the real. Whaley distinguishes between two main types of deception: simulation and dissimulation. The former is active in the sense of showing something false; the latter is aimed at hiding the real. Simulation consists in proposing a false version of reality; dissimulation withholds part of reality from the target. The final distinctions are made within the two main categories. Simulation consists of three possible procedures: mimicking—which shows the false by imitating another existing thing; inventing—by displaying another, entirely new reality; and decoying—diverting attention, creating an alternative reality. Dissimulation consists of masking—which hides the real by making it invisible; repackaging—which hides the real by disguising it, modifying its appearance; and dazzling—which hides the real by confusing, reducing certainty about the nature of the thing.

Now, the distinction between deception that misrepresents a state of affairs different from the deceptive act and deception that misrepresents the act of communication of which it is part seems to correspond with the distinctions made by Whaley (1982). Extralinguistic (for lack of a better term) deception corresponds with the category of simulation. It is an attempt to actively show an alternative reality. The speaker/deceiver proposes a false account of what he or she believes to be the case. It is predominantly, it seems, an exercise in what Whaley calls inventing. In the data that formed the basis for this analysis, extralinguistic deception consists in ascribing to the misrepresented speaker something he or she had not in fact said.

Metadiscursive deception, on the other hand, can be subsumed under the category of dissimulation. It is the speaker's attempt to conceal the uncooperativeness of her or his response. Predominantly, therefore, metadiscursive strategies involve what Whaley (1982) has called masking, linguistic devices used to make the uncooperativeness invisible. Finally, deception by omission—withholding relevant information—a category that for obvious reasons is not subsumed within the typology offered in Chapter 3, is also an act of dissimulation.

The exercise of incorporating a study of linguistic deception into a general theory of deception serves at least two purposes. First, it helps to describe linguistic categories in terms applicable to other forms of deception, and thus it also helps to frame further research in to deceptive message. Second, it reiterates that deception, regardless of its type, is always a semiotic activity; it always involves manipulation of symbols whatever their nature may be.

CONCLUDING REMARKS

The analyses presented in this chapter go beyond descriptions of metadiscursive deception and its strategies. It is argued that the framework within which the phenomenon and its subcategories were analyzed provides a frame of reference for an overall account of the linguistic workings of deceptive messages. It seems also that the analysis can be combined with earlier analyses of extralinguistic deceptive strategies and thus be part of the overall theory of deceptive communication. Furthermore, these discussions will also be examined in view of an overall theory of deception, of which linguistic deception should be a homogeneous part.

There are, however, some problems raised by this account. At the beginning of the discussion, I argued that masking devices described here are deceptive, in contrast to those discussed by Ng and Bradac (1993). The question that can be posed is this: Are all metadiscursive masks necessarily deceptive?

The case in point is that of boasting. As I have argued elsewhere (e.g., Galasiński, 1992), a number of devices are used to safeguard the speaker from the cultural sanction against overt boasting. These may include strategies such as concealing the identity of the speaker, presenting the utterance as objective, denying boastful intentions, and indicating the speaker's modesty. The function of these masks is precisely to make the utterance appear as not boastful, similar to those described above. Are these masks, or, indeed, other devices breaching the politeness principle (Leech, 1983), deceptive?

The question is difficult because masking devices of this type are partly conventionalized and as such give the game away. The addressee may well be able to recognize at least some of them as functioning precisely as mitigators of boasting. By conventionalization, such masking devices may become mitigators, and, instead of concealing the act of boasting, they soften its effect. I do not have a ready answer to the problem and prefer to leave it open for further research. There are also a number of possible acts that could be more readily described as metadiscursively deceptive. Persuasion, propaganda, innuendo, and other acts of strategic communication are likely to include devices that are aimed at passing them as nonstrategic, not attaining speakers' concealed goals. The role of this chapter, however, was to provide a framework for such analyses. The analyses themselves must be deferred to the future.

The next chapter once again shifts the perspective of the book. I shall be interested in extralinguistic deception. More particularly, I shall analyze deceptive communication as a joint cooperative endeavor between the interlocutors.

Appendix

(8)   Polish Original of Exchange

Polish version of Wałęsa's turn:

507-511:   . . . Mój kontrpartner mówi o jakiejś konfrontacji a więc szykuje NATO do wojny z kim? z Litwą prawdopodobnie bo z Rosją ma Ameryka dobre stosunki i NATO też to właściwie będziemy się zbroić i wstępować do NATO bo Litwie wojne wypowiemy? Absurd. Nie ma innego sposobu w tym momencie—

512: K: Kto to powiedział?

513: W: Ale, no, ale no jeśli się coś takiego mówi to tak to wygląda. . . .

514: K: Pan tyle zrozumiał z tego.

Polish version of Kwaśniewski's turn:

529-531:   Bardzo krótko zacznę jednak od tej Litwy. Otóż ja chcę jasno powiedzieć ani przez moment nie uważałem nie uważam i to nie wynika ze słów które tu wypowiedziałem ze nasze wejście do NATO ma być konfrontacją z kimkolwiek.

532-534:   Mówiłem wielokrotnie że to ma być element *sta*bilności a nie konfrontacji. Jeżeli ktokolwiek mnie inaczej rozumie to albo ma zła wolę albo po prostu nie chce tego zrozumieć. . . .

6

Conversation for Misrepresentation

This chapter is aimed at demonstrating how a televised conversation was used by both participants as a *joint* endeavor to show reality in a desired way. First, I shall show that both the interviewer and the interviewee *cooperated* in performing acts of misrepresentation. Second, and more generally, I shall propose that deception can be an act of cooperation. I shall argue that conversation as a whole—its overall aims—can be contingent on misrepresentation.

In the conversation to be analyzed, the construction of the dialogic exchange between the two interlocutors is ancillary to their representational attempts. Although the exchange is an interview, it is not so much geared toward extracting information—as it is normally in the case of the interviewer—or giving it—as in the case of the interviewee. Instead, it enables both parties to contribute in the endeavor of (mis)representation of reality.

Data and Context

The interview I shall analyze below comes from a Polish weekly talk show (*WC Kwadrans* [WC Quarter], hosted by Wojciech Cejrowski). The show was one of the most controversial programs on Polish public television (TVP1). The host of the show was continually accused of being systematically biased against anything that did not conform to his Catholic, nationalist, anti-Semitic, and anti-feminist views. Also, the manner in which the interviews were carried out was often strongly criticized. The interviewer usually positioned himself explicitly as an enemy or a friend of the interviewee. If the former was the case, the interview became aggressive, often insulting, aimed not to argue with but rather to attack and ridicule the interviewee. After surviving numerous cancellation attempts, the show was finally taken off the air.

The conversation I shall analyze was broadcast in September 1995. It concerns preparations of the Polish committee of nongovernmental organizations for the United Nations conference on women in Beijing. The interviewee is a representative of one of such organizations. According to her claims, her organization was not treated justly by the committee and was unlikely to be represented in Beijing. The crucial issue raised in the interview was that of the representativeness of the committee. It is here where interlocutors' violations start. Right from the start of the interview, both the interviewer and the interviewee join their forces in a negative representation of both the committee and its actions. In fact, negative presentation of the committee seemed to be the overall aim of the interview. More particularly, both interlocutors set out to undermine the representativeness of the committee, portraying it as having no right to be a representative of women's organizations or as usurping that right.

COOPERATION TO MISLEAD

I shall first discuss what I have called buildup of misrepresentations, that is, a series of stronger and stronger misrepresentations made by the interlocutors. Then I shall analyze the interviewee's acceptance of misrepresentations made by the interviewer.

Building Up Misrepresentations

Below is a fragment of the exchange in which interlocutors engage in joint misrepresentations. The quoted exchange is the interviewer's third move. Earlier in the interview, the interviewee explained that the committee had invited a number of nongovernmental organizations to take part in its work. She also complained that only two representatives of her organization could take part in the meetings. It was regarded as fostering inequality and undemocratic practices. The interviewee, however, did take part in at least one meeting (she is one of the two unaffiliated persons mentioned in A6; the other person remains unidentified throughout the interview). Consider the following. (A is the interviewer, and B is the interviewee.)

(1)

English version of the exchange:

24-28: A1:   The report in a better cover than mine, which the viewers know from the quotes in [name of the show], was given out there. This is, this is the stenciled version, and this is the new version, the Citizens'[1] Committee of the Non-Governmental Organizations, Beijing '95, and it is shown here what kind of committee is going to represent us in Beijing—several associations, mainly feminist, although not only, whose names are longer than members' lists.

29-30: Madam, is it going to be an official Polish document?! They say, they will be representing Poland?!

31-32: B1: That is, the Citizens' Committee says that it is a representative of nongovernmental organizations, only, however, as I have already said, it is a very peculiar . . .

33: B1: . . . representation because it contains only 12 nongovernmental organizations.

34-35: A2: But they are going there to represent the whole Poland?

36-37: B2: But they are going there, they claim that they will represent all the nongovernmental organizations, however. . . .

38: A3: So you too? [will be represented by them]

39: B3: You too, me too, in this situation, me too.

40-41: A4: So they will represent all organizations, even those which did not agree to that, collaborate with them and come to the meetings.

42: B4: Yes.

43-45: A5: I see. And we have already said various things about this report. So they invite undemocratically, they create some report of theirs, also undemocratically, because their own, but they will represent everybody.

46: B5: Well, they want to represent everybody.

47: A6: Madam, so they—

48-49: B6: I believe that in their report, they should write that it is a report of 12 nongovernmental organizations and two unaffiliated persons. That would be true.

The problem of representativeness is first raised by the interviewer in the two questions at the end of his first move (A1, lines 29-30). The intonation of the first question suggested that the speaker was surprised at the possibility that the committee may want to represent Poland. The interviewer's question is one of the range of the committee's representativeness. The second question is also intoned to indicate a surprise with a possibility of a positive answer.

B's response is an attempt to set the record straight, especially that the interviewer asks about the committee's own claims. Indeed, B1 focuses on the committee's claims to be a representative of nongovernmental organizations. The interviewee does not refer to the committee's representing intentions in Beijing. Furthermore, B attempts not to commit herself to a claim as to the range of the committee's representation. The Polish "is a representative of nongovernmental organizations" (*jest reprezentantem organizacji pozarzadowych*) is not indicative of how many of those organizations are "covered" by the representation; rather, it is an indication of the types of organizations that are represented, as suggested by the postnominal position of the adjective and the adverb *wyłącznie* ("only," "exclusively"). The interviewee's move is an attempt not to take up the interviewer's bid to misrepresent the group's claim to the range of representativeness.

In A2, however, the interviewer repeats the question as if he was not satisfied by the answer. The contrasting *ale* ("but") at the beginning (lines 34-35), putting the question in opposition to the answer, as well as the utterance's intonation, indicates that what is required is merely a confirmation. The questioner's attempt to elicit confirmation to his reiterated question is in effect a request to misrepresent, to make a stronger claim than is warranted by what has already been said. B actually takes up the interviewer's bid. In her second response, she makes a stronger claim than the one she had made in B1. This time, B says that the committee claims to represent *all* nongovernmental organizations. It seems to me that this is the critical juncture in the exchange—getting the interviewee to make a stronger claim is to impart the interviewer's goal of constructing a particular representation of a group of people.

In her agreement (B3), B uses a hedge ("in this situation," a somewhat inadequate translation of *w tym momencie*) to license the potential untruthfulness of her statement (cf. Mura, 1983). The phrase can be seen as an endorsement of the "argument line" proposed by the interviewer. It suggests that B does not make a statement on her own accord but, rather, accepts what is said by her conversation partner. As such, therefore, the hedge is an attempt to shift some of the responsibility for the potential misrepresentation to the interviewer. This is the first indication of the interviewee's possible discomfort in the role of an "accessory" to misrepresentation.

In A4, the interviewer continues raising the stakes with regard to the committee's alleged claim to represent all nongovernmental organizations. He brings out the assumption of representing those who did not wish to be represented, and B concurs. In A5, the interviewer states that the committee will represent *everybody*. The interviewer gets back to his initial bid to elicit B's agreement with a claim that the committee will represent the entire Poland (lines 29-30) and gets the interviewee to concur.

In the interviewee's agreement (B5), however, not only does she introduce the utterance by *no* (roughly an equivalent to initial "well"), a particle that indicates hesitation, but also she gives up the claim that the committee *claims* something; this time, she says that it *wants* something. The shift can be interpreted as moving to safer ground and avoiding potential responsibility for lying. Although it is easy to check whether the committee in general or its members in particular made or did not make a statement as to their wishes to represent someone at the conference, it is considerably more difficult to check whether they only wanted it.

The buildup is stopped by B's last remark. In B6, she returns to the issue of 12 organizations being part of the committee. B seems to have realized that she may have taken part in a series of misrepresentations and now wishes to redress it. Thus, she shifts the focus of her utterance to the committee's report.

Of particular interest about the misrepresentations is that they are elicited by the interviewer. He directs the conversation in such a way that the only choice the interviewee has is either to challenge him overtly—which, presumably, she does not want to do, given the overall aim of the interview—or to go along and cooperate making the misrepresentations. The interviewee indicates her discomfort with the accounts, however. She attempts to shift the responsibility for assertions to A (as in B3) or introduces her claims by nonfactive clauses (B5), that is, by clauses that do not introduce presuppositions, do not take things for granted. In B5, the *no* ("well") suggests a compromise between the unfolding statement and the one made by A. Finally, she interrupts A and explains how things should be put. Her actions can be seen as somewhat unwilling cooperation with the interviewer.

Accepting Misrepresentations

The dialogic cooperation with the goal of misrepresenting reality is continued a few moments later toward the end of the conversation. This time, the existence of misrepresentations is only accepted, and the misrepresentations are not used as a background to making further, stronger ones. Witness the following exchange.

(2)

English version of the exchange:

72: A7:   And who drew up the list of the women who will go?

73: B7:   They themselves, I think, because I don't know any such body which would—

74-76: A8:   Madam, but by what right does somebody send themselves? So I'll send myself as the ambassador to Israel, for example.

77-78: B8:   I think that it is neither a representation of nongovernmental organizations nor a representation of Polish women.

79-80: A9:   And did you ask them who had sent them there, who is carrying them? By what right are they, and not you, for example, going?

81-82: B9:   I asked who and how formed the committee, and I learned that a group of women who wanted to go to Beijing gathered.

83-85: A10:   You ladies could have used the same method, invite two feminists and 300 persons from other organizations, call such a thing, write blue papers, create a list, write for invitations not to New York but to Moscow, and go to Beijing.

86-87:   Who is doing it? Because if you could not do such a thing, but they could, then where is the key to it?

88: B10:   Well, I would like to know myself.

In the first two moves (A7 and B7), the interlocutors are preparing ground for the forthcoming misrepresentations. The interviewer asks a straightforward question and receives a relevant answer. The answer is perfectly justifiable—the hedge *chyba* (a particle with a function similar to that of "I think," yet without a reference to a mental process) lifts the assertion of B's claim and makes it "safe." B goes even further than hedging; she gives reasons for saying what she said, making her utterance more credible.

Now, the interviewer's second question (A8) carries a misrepresentation. He presupposes that some persons are sending themselves, and by a conversational implication (maxim of manner is flouted by the use of ambiguous *ktoś,* "somebody"), he disambiguates the presupposition, implying that it is the women in the committee. The misrepresentation not only is carried by the implied part of the utterance but also is made to be evidenced by the interviewee's words. The question is introduced by the conjunction *ale* ("but") and thus made to be directly linked with B's answer (B7). In fact, however, B7 does not warrant the interviewer's implication. Although B qualified it, A, by putting it into a presupposition, shows the "self-sending" as an established fact. Furthermore, and even more important, by his rhetorical question, the interviewer implicates that the people in general (and thus the committee in particular) have no right to send themselves to the conference. The implicature is then "corroborated" by the implicature in A's next statement: He obviously cannot send himself as the ambassador to Israel.[2]

The interviewee's next move (B8) hardly contributes to the flow of the conversation. To be fully cooperative, she must either challenge the interviewer or, alternatively, endorse the misrepresentation. The third option is noncooperation, yet one that is not visible or cannot be construed as a challenge. Indeed, her utterance, although retaining the overall topic of the exchange, is merely a statement of B's position toward the committee's representativeness. The interviewer's response to that is an introduction of a new issue signaled by the initial *a* (somewhat similar to "and" yet more readily indicating an introduction of a new topic).

CONCLUDING REMARKS

The above analysis was aimed at demonstrating that misrepresentations cannot be understood simply as acts of noncooperation. The analysis of the above exchanges showed that misrepresentations were cooperative in view of the overall flow of the exchange: the negative presentation of an organization. As has been shown above, the interlocutors were engaged in what could be seen, at the least, as building up the grounds for a final misrepresentation, or simply a buildup of misrepresentations. In the second exchange, misrepresentations were accepted as part of the exchange. The interlocutors could be seen as cooperating in constructing a certain picture of reality that previous discourse shows to be a misrepresentation.

Cooperation in the debate has at least two levels. The interviewer and the interviewee cooperate on the basic level: Their conversation is continued throughout the show; they are also comprehensible to each other and to the audience, the licensed participant of the communicative situation (cf. Clark & Carlson, 1982; see also Clark, 1987). The interlocutors also cooperate on at least two other levels, however. They cooperate in *misrepresenting* and *accepting* misrepresentation. Finally, their cooperation has the additional dimension of the relationship with the audience. They cooperate in being *uncooperative* toward the audience. If the default expectation is observance of the maxims of conversation, then the two speakers are colluding in not revealing the fact of misrepresentations.

One final point can be made with respect to this study. The cooperation in misrepresenting cannot be seen without reference to the problems of discursive representation. As has been indicated throughout the chapter, the overall aim of the interview was the negative presentation of the Citizens' Committee of Non-Governmental Organizations, Beijing '95. The misrepresentation occurred in at least two levels: dialogic cooperation (making and accepting misrepresentations) and the level of discursive representations, such as, for example, the interlocutors' lexical choices. Misrepresentation can be seen here as one of the superstrategies of constructing a certain picture of extralinguistic reality and as ancillary to the overall representational aims of the speakers.

The next chapter draws together the discussions of extralinguistic and metadiscursive deception. It is an attempt to sketch the pragmatics of deception. I shall therefore be asking questions of the communicative functions of acts of deception.

Appendix

(1)

Polish original of exchange:

24-28: A1:   Tam rozdawano w lepszej obwolucie niż moja raport który państwo już znają z cytatów z [name of the show]. Oto on to jest wersja powielaczowa stara a tu jest wersja nowa Społeczny Komitet Organizacji Pozarządowych Pekin 95 no i tu jest pokazane co to za komitet będzie nas w Pekinie reprezentował. Kilkanaście stowarzyszeń feministycznych głównie choć nie tylko których nazwy sa dłuższe od listy członków.

29-30:   Proszę pani, to oficjalny polski dokument będzie? One mówią że będą Polskę reprezentować?

31-33: B1:   To znaczy Społeczny Komitet mówi że jest reprezentantem organizacji pozarządowcyh wyłącznie niemniej jednak jak już powiedziałam jest to specyficzna reprezentacja bo zawiera tylko listę 12 organizacji
⎡ pozarządowych—
34-35: A2:   ⎣ Ale będą jechać reprezentować całą Polskę?

36-37: B2:   Ale będą jechać one twierdzą że będą reprezentować wszystkie organizacje pozarządowe niemniej jednak—

38: A3:   To panią również?

39: B3:   Panią mnie również w tym momencie mnie również.

40-41: A4:   Czyli będą reprezentować wszystkie organizacje nawet te które się na to nie zgodziły kolaborować z nimi i przychodzić na spotkania?

42: B4:   Tak.

43-45: A5:   Aaaa. A o tym raporcie już mówiliśmy różne rzeczy no więc tak: zapraszają niedemokratycznie tworzą jakiś swój raport też niedemokratycznie bo swój własny, ale reprezentować będą wszystkich.

46: B5:   No, chcą reprezentować wszystkich.

47: A6:   Proszę pani, to one—

48-49: B6:   Uważam że powinny w swoim raporcie napisać że jest to raport organizacji pozarządowych plus dwu osób niezrzeszonych. To by była prawda.

(2)

Polish original of exchange:

72: A7:   A kto ustalił listę kobiet które pojadą?

73: B7:   One same, chyba, bo ja nie znam żadnego gremium które by—

74-76: A8:   Proszę pani, ale jakim prawem sam się ktoś wysyla? To ja się zaraz wyślę na ambasadora do Izraela na przykład.

77-78: B8:   Uważam że nie jest to ani reprezentacja organizacji pozarządowych ani reprezentacja kobiet polskich.

79-80: A9:   A zapytala pani kto je tam posłał kto je niesie? Jakim prawem one a nie pani jadą na przykład?

81-82: B9:   Zapytałam kto formułował i jak formułował się ten komitet i dowiedziałam się że zebrała się grupa kobiet które chciały jechać do Pekinu.

83-85: A10:   Mogly panie zastosować podobną metodę, zaprosić dwie feministki i 300 osób z innych organizacji zwołać takie coś niebieskie papierki napisać stworzyć listę nie do Nowego Jorku, tylko do Moskwy napisać o zaproszenia i pojechać do Pekinu.

86-87:   Kto to niesie? No bo jak pani nie mogła czegoś takiego zrobić tylko one mogły to gdzie jest, proszę pani, klucz do tego?

88: B10:   No, też chciałabym wiedzieć.

NOTES

1. A note on translation is due here. I have translated Polish *społeczny* in the name of the committee as "citizens," although it is normally rendered as "social." The Polish word is used here to indicate that the committee was independent of any political or governmental organization.

Throughout the fragment, "they" in the English translation refers to Polish *one*, which is also third person plural yet has feminine gender, that is, can refer only to women.

2. The choice of the country is also important here. As I signaled above, the show in general was often blamed for its nationalism and anti-Semitism. The implicature therefore gets strengthened by this reference—even if he could send himself—Israel is the least likely destination.

Furthermore, the interviewer puts the committee on a par with representatives of the country and the government. Such positioning is also misleading. There is no reason to assume that a group of women cannot simply decide to go wherever they choose, especially if they are not funded by the taxpayer's money (the interviewer calls their funds "some money"). The source of the committee's funding is in fact never addressed.

7

Pragmatics of Deception

In this chapter, I am interested in the pragmatic workings of the deceptive message. Focusing on lying and evasion, I shall analyze their functions as units of linguistic communication. I have decided to focus on lying because it can be thought of as the most typical deceptive strategy. As I indicated in Chapter 3, a number of studies into deceptive communication assume that deception can be equated with lying (see Hopper & Bell, 1984). Furthermore, lying is aimed at misrepresenting extralinguistic reality. The goal of deceptiveness of evasion, on the other hand, is to misrepresent the evasive utterance. In further contrast to lying, evasion is necessarily dialogic—there is no evasion without a (at least implicit) question-answer exchange. The juxtaposition of the two so different acts of deception, it seems, can provide insights into the variety and nature of deceptive communication.

Lying

Let me briefly recall the discussion of problems with the definition of lying (see also Shibles, 1988). In contrast to the intuitive definition of lies as false messages, Bradac (1983) describes a lie as a message constructed in such a way that the speaker believes that the addressee will believe that the speaker believes "A," whereas in fact, the speaker believes "not-A." Such an approach shows that lying is related not so much to falsity of information but, rather, to the speaker's beliefs. It does not matter whether the statement is or is not false, as long as the speaker believes it to be false. It is the intention to lie and the speaker's beliefs about reality that are constitutive of lying. Lies are *statements* that the speaker *believes to be false* and that are *intended to mislead* the addressee (cf. also Bok, 1978).

Evasion

Again, briefly, evasion is necessarily *dialogic;* second, evasive utterances are those that are *semantically irrelevant* to the questions to which they are a response; third, their irrelevance is *intentional.* Evasive actions can be *overt* and *covert.* In the case of the former, the speaker more or less explicitly signals to the hearer that he or she is not prepared to answer the question posed. In the case of covert evasion, the evader only pretends to give a cooperative answer. As in previous chapters, I shall be interested only in covert evasion.

MENDACIOUS STATEMENTS

A liar sets out to make the target believe something that he or she believes to be false. To lie, the speaker must issue an utterance that will count as a statement. In such a way, the speaker will pretend to commit to the veracity of the proposition included in the statement (cf. Searle, 1969). This is one of the felicity conditions of statements, and, on the other hand, this is the requirement put on the speaker by Grice's (1975) cooperative principle in general and the maxim of quality—truthfulness—in particular.

Issuing a false statement with the intention to deceive the target, the liar must have at least two goals. First, the liar wants the target to take the utterance as a statement and the speaker as committing her- or himself to the truth of what is said. To be deceived, the addressee must recognize the utterance as a statement, that is, an utterance that is intended to give information about reality. As in nonmisleading statements, the speaker's conventional goal is to get the addressee to become aware of a particular state of affairs. Second, the deceiver wants the target to actually believe in what is said, that is, to take the statement as an accurate representation of reality. The success of the lie is contingent on the attainment of these two goals.

Searle (1979) posits that a speaker who performs an assertion must follow the following rules: commit to the truth of the proposition (essential rule); have evidence or reasons for saying what he or she is saying, and the expressed proposition must not be obvious to either the speaker or the addressee (preparatory rule); and, finally, commit to a belief that the expressed proposition is true (sincerity rule; cf. also Reboul, 1994). The liar, therefore, not only violates the sincerity rule, as Reboul suggests, but in fact, apart from one of the preparatory conditions (the condition of nonobviousness of the statement), violates all of them. Yet the liar's goal is to issue an utterance that will pretend not to violate any. To be successful, a lie must look as if it is a mere statement. Indeed, this is why in a recent study of patient deception, Burgoon, Hunsaker, and Dawson (1994) show that outright lies are more difficult to detect solely on the basis of any language markers.

Reboul (1994) argues that lies are utterances that correspond to the performance of an act that has a sincerity condition, except that the sincerity rule was not complied with and the speaker has the intention that the addressee believe that the sincerity condition is met. This analysis leads her to accept that an insincere promise is a lie. Yet apart from the additional (higher-order) goal of deception, the speaker pursues the same goals in the case of a lie as in the case of a statement. Occam's razor, it seems, precludes the possible introduction of a new category: the speech act of a lie. Lies are no more than mendacious statements, statements that are insincere.

PRAGMATICS OF EVASION

Irrelevance of Content

To analyze the mechanism of the deceptiveness of evasion and describe it pragmatically, let us take a look at an exchange, now a classic of British television journalism, between Jeremy Paxman and former Tory Home Secretary Michael Howard, M.P. The exchange is part of the interview broadcast on BBC2's *Newsnight* on May 13, 1999. The fragment of interest here concerns the sacking of the director-general of the British prison service, Derek Lewis, and, more particularly, the questions of whether Mr. Howard did or did not threaten to overrule the director's decision not to dismiss the governor of a British prison from which inmates had escaped (JP = Jeremy Paxman; MH = Michael Howard).

JP1: Mr. Howard, did you ever lie in any public statement?

MH1: Certainly not. I gave a very full account of the dismissal of Derek Lewis to the House of Commons Select Committee, and to the House of Commons itself in a debate that took place. There can have been few decisions that have been subjected to more close and minute scrutiny in recent years than that decision. It was, it was a decision that it was necessary for me to take after terrorists had escaped from Whitemoor [prison], other dangerous prisoners had escaped from Parkhurst [prison], and an independent report had found that there were serious weaknesses in the management of the prison service from top to bottom.

JP2: Is there anything you would wish to change about your statement to the, to the House of Commons, or any other public statement you made about this matter?

MH2: No. Nothing.

JP3: Not a word.

MH3: I gave a full account of what had happened in relation to my decision.

JP4:   Right. Can you help us with this, then. You state in your statement that [*reading out*] "the leader of the opposition had said that I"—that is you—"personally told Mr. Lewis that the governor should be suspended immediately, that when Mr. Lewis objected—as it was an operational matter—I threatened to instruct him to do it." Derek Lewis says, "Howard had certainly told me that the governor at Parkhurst should be suspended and had threatened to overrule me." Are you saying that Mr. Lewis is lying?

MH4:   I have given a full account of this. And the position is what I told the House of Commons. And let me tell you what the position is—

JP5:   So you are saying that Mr. Lewis is lying?

MH5:   Let me tell you exactly what the position is. I was entitled to be consulted—

JP6:   Yes.

MH6:   And I was consulted. I was entitled to express an opinion. I did express an opinion. I was not entitled to instruct Derek Lewis what to do, and I did not instruct him what to do.

JP7:   Well, here's—

MH7:   [*overrides him*] And you will understand and recall that Mr. Marriott was not suspended. He was moved, and Derek Lewis told the select committee of the House of Commons that it was his opinion—Derek Lewis's opinion—that he should be moved immediately. That is what happened.

JP8:   Mr. Lewis says—"I"—that is, Mr. Lewis—"told him what we had decided about Marriott and why. He"—that is you—"exploded, simply proving the governor was politically unpalatable, it sounded indecisive, it would be seen as fudge. If I did not change my mind and suspend Marriott, he would have to consider overruling me."

MH8:   Mr. Marriott—

JP9:   You can't both be right.

MH9:   Mr. Marriott was not suspended. I was entitled to express my views. I was entitled to be consulted—

JP10:   Did you threaten to overrule him?

MH10:   I was, I was not entitled to instruct Derek Lewis, and I did not instruct him. And ⌈ the truth—

JP11:   ⌊ Did you threaten to overrule him?

MH11:   The truth of the matter is that Mr. Marriott was not suspended.

JP12:   ⌈ Did you threaten to overrule him?

MH12:   ⌊ I did not, I did not overrule Derek Lewis.

JP13: Did you threaten to overrule him?

MH13: I took advice on what I could and could not do.

JP14: ⌈ Did you threaten to overrule him, Mr. Howard?]

MH14: ⌊ and I acted scrupulously in accordance with that advice. I did not overrule
⌈ Derek Lewis.

JP15: ⌊ Did you *threaten* to overrule him?

MH15: Mr. Marriott was not suspended.

JP16: Did you *threaten* to overrule him?

MH16: I have accounted for my decision to dismiss Derek Lewis—

JP17: ⌈ Did you threaten to overrule him?

MH17: ⌊ —in great detail before the House of Commons.

JP18: I know. You are not answering the question whether you threatened to
overrule him.

MH18: Well, the important aspect of this, which is very clear to bear in mind—

JP19: —I'm sorry I'm gonna be frightfully rude, but—

MH19: Yes. Yes you can.

JP20: But I am sorry, but it's a question—it's a straight yes or no.

MH20: ⌈ And I will give you—I will give you an answer

JP21: ⌊ Did you threaten to overrule him? Did you threaten to overrule him?

MH21: I discussed this matter with Derek Lewis. I gave him the benefit of my
opinion. I gave him the benefit of my opinion in strong language. But I did not instruct him, because I was not entitled to instruct him. I was entitled to express my
opinion, and that is what I did.

JP22: With respect. That is not answering the question of whether you threatened
to overrule him.

MH22: It's dealing with the relevant point. Which is what I was entitled to do, and
what I was not entitled to do. And I have dealt with this in detail before the House
of Commons and before the select committee.

JP23: With respect. You haven't answered the question whether you threatened to
overrule him.

MH23: Well, you see, the question is what was I entitled to do and what was I not entitled to do. I was not entitled to instruct him, and I did not do that.

JP24: Right. We'll leave, we'll leave that aspect there.

Now, I suggest here that the truth or falsity of the answers given by Mr. Howard is irrelevant. In other words, an evading speaker is uninterested in the success of the statement he or she makes while evading an answer. The evader's goal (in the exchange above, unsuccessful) is, rather, to get the questioner to believe that the utterance is a relevant answer. The veracity of the answer is not an issue in the case of evasion; it is irrelevant at the level of the question-answer exchange (cf. also Ng & Bradac, 1993). In addition, the answers given by Howard are more or less in the public domain and are likely to be known to Paxman. In fact, the interviewer does not even engage with the content of Howard's answers.

Furthermore, the potential discovery that the answerer does not believe in what he or she says may simply rouse the interlocutor's suspicion and thus possibly make her or him more vigilant as to the flow of discourse, but it may also provide a point on which to challenge the answerer. Even if the questioner does challenge the speaker's utterance on its veracity, for example, by saying, "You don't really believe what you're saying, do you?" the challenge will operate at the level of the utterance (proposition) rather than the question-answer exchange. It would be a challenge concerning a type of uncooperativeness different from that of which the evader would be accused, and, in the process, the evader may get away with not answering the question even more easily. Moreover, such a challenge in the exchange would actually get the interviewee off the hook—the interviewer would have stopped the hammering and would not have repeated his question 14 times!

As I signaled, the exchange above is also an example of unsuccessful evasion. Jeremy Paxman, renowned to be one of the BBC's toughest interviewers, does not let Michael Howard get away with evasion, although he finally gives in and shifts the topic. More recently, the attempts of a minister, this time from the new Labour government, to evade a question three times resulted in Paxman's putting an abrupt end to the interview and Paxman's moving on with the program.

Irrelevance of the Success

If the truth of the proposition in the evader's utterance is irrelevant, it follows that in an act of evasion, the speaker is not interested in the success of her or his speech act. If issuing a statement, the speaker wants to get the addressee to realize a particular state of affairs, then the evader is not really interested in it. It is, however, possible to envisage a situation in which the appropriate answer is not a statement but, for example, a promise. Consider the following contrived example.

(1)

A: Do you promise we'll go to the cinema this week?

B: I promise we'll go out this week.

It is difficult to assess to what extent the speaker actually commits her- or himself to doing anything. Promises, to be felicitous, must be wanted and, admittedly, A does not want, or at least has not asked for, the promise he or she gets. The speaker, therefore, may well not be interested in the uptake, as long as A is prepared to accept B's utterance as a cooperative answer.

That is not to say, however, that the speaker/evader is not interested at all in how the addressee perceives the response. The evader is interested in issuing an utterance that satisfies the conversational demand pragmatically. It is also essential for the evader to get the questioner to believe that it is cooperative, thus that a pragmatically relevant statement is also relevant semantically. In other words, the speaker must appear to satisfy what Searle (1969) called the essential condition of speech acts. The speaker must send an utterance that will count as a certain speech act: a statement, a promise, or whatever other act demanded by the questioner. Finally, although the act must be—or at least appear to be—felicitous, its success, in the sense of achieving a potential effect (cf. Galasiński, 1994b), is irrelevant.

Once again, there is a difference between lies and evasion. The liar's goal to deceive depends on the success of the statement he or she makes. In the case of an evasive utterance, the success of the speech act is immaterial to the success of evasion because evasion is a *faculty* of a response, rather than a type of speech act. The speaker/evader sets out to issue an utterance with a certain force and also to use this utterance as a means to appear cooperative. The only difference is that just as in the case of a lie, certain conditions that normally obtain for the performance of utterances counting as a certain act are not satisfied. The statements used to evade are still statements, yet made insincerely. They are intended, however, to be perceived as fully felicitous.

Phatic Function of Evasion

The speaker's lack of interest in the success of her or his utterance and the irrelevance of its contents render evasion a very particular type of communicative action. Evasion seems to perform a phatic function, that is, the evasion's main function is focused on maintaining the contact between the speaker and the addressee (on phatic function, see Jakobson, 1960). If the content of the utterance is significant only insofar as appearing to be semantically relevant, what really matters is that the speaker said something at all. Evading a question is a means of controlling the flow of conversation, but at a more basic level, evasion is also a means of furthering conversation—keeping it alive, so to speak. This particular feature of evasion makes it similar to small talk, one of few communicative endeavors in which it is more important that words have been spoken rather than what has been said (Knapp & Vangelisti, 1992). There is, of course, one significant difference between the two. Irrelevance of the content of small talk is acknowledged and agreed on by both communicators; in the case of evasive responses, the target cannot be aware of the fact.

EVASION: AGENCY AND RESPONSIBILITY

I have argued above that the content of an evasive utterance is irrelevant to the speaker's attempts to evade a question successfully. Furthermore, the commitment to the truth of the proposition in an evasive statement is also irrelevant to the success of the speaker's evasive action. Taking this argument one step further results in a claim that the speaker does not have to be responsible for what he or she says. Even intuitively, however, such a claim seems wrong. It is plausible to assume that there are no circumstances in which speakers are free to say whatever they want and get away with it. In Halliday's (1978) words, there are no fully open registers. Although evasion does cancel the speaker's commitment communicatively, the form of the assertive utterance will still convey some form of commitment to the proposition included within it.

The evader is faced with a potential conflict, then. On the one hand, given the irrelevance of the content of the evasive utterance, the evader is free to use the utterance strategically and make it appear relevant to the question. On the other hand, however, the strategic use of the utterance may prove counterproductive relative to the necessary commitment to the proposition that the form of the utterance forces the speaker to make. The way out of the problem involves two options: either to make the response safe (regarding the overall communicative and political strategy) or, alternatively, to waive any responsibility for the claim made.

The analysis that I shall present below is aimed at testing this hypothesis. I shall attempt to ask the question of what it is, in the linguistic form, that evasive speakers commit themselves to, and what type of statements they use when engaging in evasion. The analysis draws on the developments of Halliday's (1994) functional linguistics. Its main tenet is that the analysis of lexico-grammatical form of utterances should be foregrounded as a resource for constructing meaning. Elements of grammar and lexis are analyzed predominantly as having a particular function when used by speakers. I shall also draw on the developments of critical linguistics and critical discourse analysis (cf., e.g., Caldas-Coulthard & Coulthard, 1996; Chouliaraki & Fairclough, 1999; Fairclough, 1989, 1992, 1995; Fowler, Hodge, Kress, & Trew, 1979; Hodge & Kress, 1993; Kress, 1991; van Dijk, 1991) that assumed a link between the linguistic form and social and political activity (Chilton & Schaeffner, 1997). In the analysis below, I am primarily interested in who is positioned as a participant in the processes referred to in the response and what type of actions or states are attributed to them.

The analysis will show that in their linguistic content, there are four overlapping and jointly used types of evasive answers. Speakers (a) put themselves in a position of an agent in a mental process, (b) referred to their more or less widely known activities, (c) stated what they will *not* do, and (d) made a generic statement, the truth of which could be taken for granted.

Mental Processes

The first of the categories distinguished includes utterances in which the speaker puts her- or himself in a position of an agent in a mental process (see Halliday, 1994; Simpson, 1993). The speaker/answerer presents her- or himself as being (or having been) of an opinion, thinking something, and so on. Witness the following.

(2)

A: You will not predict that you will keep it. You're only saying that you aim to keep it?

B: *We wish to keep it, we believe that we will keep it,* but there is very little margin of room for maneuver here.

(3)

A: Would a two-tier Europe actually be a good idea in some ways?

B: *I think we want* to remain in the mainstream of Europe. *It must be* in this country's interest that we participate in the important decisions in Europe, because they will profoundly affect us. *And we don't want* a Europe that is just dominated by only France and Germany.

In the two examples, evaders resort to similar tactics not to say anything about the outside world. The mental clauses introducing their statements change the referents from the speakers to their state of mind. Their statements are at best hypotheses (cf. Grzegorczykowa, 1990), rather than declarations about the world. This is also why Brown and Levinson (1987) describe such expressions as *hedges,* roughly, devices that qualify what is being said (see also McLaughlin, 1984). More particularly, clauses referring to mental processes are described as hedges on Gricean maxims, in other words, expressions that modify the operation of maxims of conversation or license their violation (Mura, 1983).

In (3), B refers to a volitional state, introducing it with a clause already referring to a state of mind. B makes a hypothesis about B's own opinions and wishes. The device clearly is aiming at softening the strength of the claim.

Negative Action

The second strategy consists of utterances in which the speaker presents her- or himself as *not doing* something.

(4)

A: Will you make a pledge tonight below which, an income level that you will not go below? I am looking for numbers, sir, not just the concept.

B: ... I can tell you this. *I will not raise taxes* on the middle class to pay for these programs.

(5)

A: You're saying that there will be nobody who is poor and working who will not be seriously inconvenienced . . . by this [increase of prescription charges]?

B: I think it's perfectly legitimate to have a debate around this subject. What *I won't do,* if you forgive me, is take lessons from Tessa and Charles, bearing in mind that both their manifestos on which their parties lost the last election were quite clearly and explicitly in favor of prescription charges and charges within NHS.

Although saying that one will not do something may be an indication of what one will do, that is hardly the case in the exchanges above. Not intending to raise taxes on a particular social group to pay for particular programs does not mean that taxes will not be raised, and the statement offers little insight into potential presidential actions. Similarly, not taking lessons from somebody does not mean that their views are not accepted. Evaders offer nothing that indicates their action or plans.

Self- and Other-Presentation

Evaders may also make references to activities that can be assumed to be commonly known. Alternatively, these may be references to activities that result in an obvious way from the speaker's job or, so to speak, the "nature of the world." Particularly when the speaker refers to her- or himself, these references are positive. Consider the following examples of self-presentation.

(6)

A: Where do you stand on gun control, and what do you plan to do about it?

B: I think you put your finger on a major problem. *I talk about strengthening the American family,* and it's very hard to strengthen the family if people are scared to walk down to the corner store and, you know, send their children down to get a loaf of bread. It's very hard. *I have been fighting for a very strong anticrime legislation,* habeas corpus reform, so you don't have those endless appeals, so when somebody gets sentenced, hey, this is for real. . . .

(7)

A: If you had to do it over again, would you put on the nation's uniform, and, if elected, could you in good conscience send someone to war?

B: If I had to do it over again, I might answer your question better. You know, *I have been in public life* a long time, and *no one had ever questioned my role,* and *I was asked* a lot of questions about things that happened a long time ago, and I don't think *I answered* them as well as I could have. . . .

I decided to classify the clause introduced by *no one* in (7) within the category of self-presentation because B describes himself through the actions of others. It is one of the potential techniques of masked self-presentation (cf. Galasiński, 1992).

As I signaled above, the answerers cannot be said to reveal any new information. Their utterances, which presumably also have a persuasive function, are stating things that are known or can be known to any interested follower of the political life. The speakers do not put themselves at any risk by making such assertions.

The same comments can be made in reference to other-presentation. Witness the following examples of other-presentation in the exchanges below.

(8)

A: Is the emissary going to Northern Ireland? . . . Is he a peace envoy, or is he on a fact-finding mission, and does it matter?

B: Obviously, the president and the prime minister *talked about this. The president is interested, is considering* the idea of appointing a representative on a fact-finding mission.

(9)

A1: The management of it [the Maastricht treaty in the Parliament] has been incompetent beyond belief, hasn't it?

B1: I think that is a very easy thing to say. And I think that *the government with the benefit of hindsight would do* a number of things differently. . . .

A2: The trouble is these chaps are not very good at it [governing]. They don't act to quote you in a way which is sensible, because they're incompetent.

B2:   Well, as I say, we're enjoying the benefit of hindsight. *They've done a number of things* which at the time must have seemed worthwhile . . . which have actually backfired.

It is any president's or prime minister's job to talk about issues such as the role of a presidential emissary. In the same way, a statement as to what the president is considering or what the president is interested in is hardly a definitive answer as to what is going to happen, although it might imply it. The reference to the two mental processes ascribed to the president allows easy denial of the implication. The same comment applies to the exchanges in (9). It is obvious that things are done because they seem worthwhile, and if they don't work out—given the chance—they would be changed. But then if the speaker is a chairman of the party whose government is under attack, there is hardly more he or she can actually say.

General Truths

The final strategy employed by evaders consists in making a statement about the nature of the world. The statements in question can have the form of a generic statement whose truth is normally not debatable (e.g., Fowler, 1991) or can be an expression of truth in a particular situation. The statements can be about both the extralinguistic reality and the world of values, for example, referring to what needs or does not need to be done. Witness the following exchange.

(10)

A: What's your acceptable minimum [of unemployment]? . . . Knocking a million off would be OK?

B: . . . Of course *one would, what one wants to see* is unemployment as low as it can possibly go. I don't know what the ultimate capacity of work for people would be in this country. I would think Sir Bryan would know much better than I do. But what *we need to do* is to ensure that when these jobs do pick up, as they did in the boom of the '80s, regardless of what mistakes were made during that time, *there was a huge surge* of employment, *we need to create* conditions of the sustained growth. . . . So *I don't think there is* a minimum level; *there is* a desirable level. . . .

(11)

A: Why wasn't it [prescription charges increase] in line with inflation?

B: *There is no commitment by any government or any political party* that it will never increase or decrease anything by more than the rate of inflation. . . .

Similarly to the previous strategy, also here the speakers choose to give a "safe" response. Making a general claim, the speaker acknowledges only the existence of a rule, principle, law, and so on. Although such statements may imply a position of power (cf. Fowler, 1991)—after all, the speaker assumes the role of someone who is able (knowledgeable or experienced enough) to "reveal the nature of the world"—the statements do not commit the speaker to doing anything or even having any particular views. Statements expressing some general truths are proverbial rather than debatable; they are a matter of common sense.

RESPONSIBILITY

Evasive speakers resort to four strategies when responding. They put themselves in a position of an agent in a mental process, refer to their commonly known activities, indicate what they did not or will not do, and make generic statements about the nature of the world. Speakers' responses were either weak in commitment or lacked informativeness. The results confirm the hypothesis I made at the outset of the analysis. Claims made in evasive utterances not only are irrelevant to the answered questions but also put their authors under no or little responsibility when claiming them. Evasive speakers can hardly be challenged for making such statements. Thus, an evader not only does not have to be responsible for what he or she says—which is, as I argued earlier, the pragmatic nature of evasive utterances—but also, when evading, actually makes claims, accountability for which is unproblematic. They do not render the speaker committed to the truth of propositions about the world as we *don't know it*—which seems to be the main point of an informative statement.

PRAGMATICS OF DECEPTION

I have come to the point when I can attempt to ask the question of what is deceptive communication as seen by a linguist. Is it a type of speech act, a kind of activity, or a genre in which users of language engage? It seems that the basic answer to such a question is that deceptive communication is *parasitic* (Reboul, 1994) on nondeceptive communication. For the deceiver to succeed in an attempt to get the addressee to believe something, the deceiver must pretend to issue a sincere utterance, a speech act of some sort. Furthermore, the success of that speech act—as is in the case of a lie—may be crucial to attaining the speaker's deceptive goal. But all that reasoning does not yet describe the deceptive act itself. What does the deceiver do, linguistically speaking, when he or she attempts to fool the addressee? What is an act of parasitic communication?

In his study of innuendo, Bell (1997) sets out to analyze it relative to pragmatic acts. He borrows the notion of the pragmatic act from Mey (1993), who describes it as all those linguistic acts in which speakers convey the message not by the codified formula of a speech act—a promise, an order, and so forth—but, rather, by a range of possibilities that can be described as hints, prompts, or innuendoes (Bell, 1997). Bell takes up the notion and uses it as a means of distinguishing between nonovert and overt acts of communication and, still following Mey, goes on to ascribe three main features to them: nonovertness, their contextual rootedness, and their deniability. Innuendo, according to Bell, is a pragmatic act. It involves a nonovert intent of the speaker, one that the addressee of the innuendo cannot be aware of. Context-dependent, its intention can also be denied.

It seems that this framework is also useful with regard to deceptive communication. An act of deception is a pragmatic act. It always contains an overt and a covert element. More specifically, an act of deception relies on the nonovert use of speech acts. Deceptive utterances differ in the way they exploit the act used to further deceptive goals. As in falsehoods (e.g., lies), the deceiver relies on the success of the statement in getting the addressee to believe something false. This, it seems, is the case of all extralinguistic deception.

Covert evasion, on the other hand, is different. The success of the act used in evading a question covertly is irrelevant insofar as the act of evasion is concerned. At the most, it may be used to conceal evasion better and allow the speaker not to commit her- or himself to evasive utterances. This seems to be true of metadiscursive strategies of deception in general. For example, the success of the explicit speech act used to carry an implicit misrepresentation seems irrelevant from the view of deceiving the addressee. In this case, however, the matter is more complicated because this particular speech act, together with its implicit part, is also used in an act of extralinguistic deception (see Chapter 3). More generally, deception uses communication to maintain the appearances of being cooperative.

Finally, Bell's (1997) study of innuendo, coupled with the proposals made above, provides a good basis for the analysis of linguistic manipulation in general. Innuendo may, but may not be, an act of (metadiscursive) deception. It is, however, an act of manipulation—an act, as I pointed out in Chapter 2, that is aimed at getting the target to do or to believe something in a covert, clandestine way (cf. Puzynina, 1992). Linguistic manipulation is also a pragmatic act that is carried out by the use of a seemingly cooperative speech act.

CONCLUDING REMARKS

The objective of this chapter was twofold. First, it was to lay out the foundations of the pragmatic description of deceptive communication. In the first instance, I attempted to do it by reference to lying and evasion. I argued that neither of the deceptive acts can be thought of as a type of speech act (with a distinct force, conventional goal, and propositional content). Lies are statements that are mendacious; evasiveness is an attribute of an utterance used as a response.

The discussion of the pragmatic nature of evasion was corroborated by a functional analysis. I confirmed the hypothesis that evasive speakers will either make their response safe or waive responsibility for the claim made. The results of the analysis showed that evaders either hedged their responses or equipped them with uninformative contents. Second, I proposed to analyze deception as a pragmatic act: a nonovert act of communication that relies on the performance of another act, one that appears to be cooperative.

The end of this chapter marks the end of the route through the many aspects of deceptive communication for the linguist—me!—trying to say something about how people use language to deceive each other. In the concluding chapter, I shall offer a summary of the most important points in this book. But I shall also briefly sketch some possible avenues for future research into the deceptive message. More particularly, I shall cast my linguistic eye beyond the realm of language and offer some comments on the deceptiveness of the visual message.

8

Conclusions
A Linguist's Look Beyond Language

THREE GOOD THINGS ABOUT THE BOOK

The way to structure texts, apparently, is to follow the rule: "Tell them what you are going to tell them, tell them, and then tell them what you have told them." This book is going to be no different. Still, having finished the last chapter, I started wondering what I should put in the conclusions. I thought that going through the different arguments of the discussion would be tedious and repetitive; all those readers who are interested enough to come all this way through the book are likely to have noted those things.

I thought, therefore, that perhaps I should follow the telling-it-thrice rule but in a different—not to say, deceptive—way. I thought that I should point out in the final chapter the three things that I would like the reader of the book— whether an academic, a student, or a person interested in the not-so-innocuous workings of the language—to remember.

Real Deceptions

The first thing that I would like to remind my readers of is that what they have read in the book was not based on my attempts to construct for myself a nice database of utterances that I have paid some people to come up with. The first good thing about this book is that all ideas I came up with regarding deception were based on how real people spoke in real life (provided, of course, that we agree on a potentially controversial thesis that politics and politicians have anything to do with real life). I have not asked anyone to lie to me or to evade my questions. Rather, I came up with an idea of analyzing deception as an attempt to misrepresent previous discourse within the same communicative situation. In such a way, I based my analysis on how debaters misrepresented other debaters' contributions.

This approach is not ideal. It does not deal with the problem of intention—it is impossible to find out empirically whether a speaker did or did not attempt to be deceptive. Of course, I realize that it is possible to ask people what their intentions were. Even with their good will and cooperation, however, their answers will refer to what they perceived, remembered, or thought their intentions were. One could also ask people, the bystanders, to judge whether what they heard was an act of deception, but then one would have to admit that perceived deception has some upper hand over the intended (actual?) one. Finally, I am not interested here in what many people think of a message; I am interested in analyzing it using some methods.

What is just about possible, however, is to see how misrepresentation serves certain overall discursive strategies of representing reality in a particular way. Deception seems to be conducive to such representations.

The all-linguistic data, of course, do not have to come only from political debates. It seems that many communicative situations in which language is represented might be potentially interesting from the view of research into deception, especially when one is faced with such interviews as the famous televised conversation between Princess Diana and Martin Bashir, full of implications, hints, and half-admissions (cf. e.g., Bull, 1997). With the audience in excess of 20 million people, the interview was covered the following day in all British media, which exceeded each other in interpreting her utterances in all possible sorts of ways (see Galasiński, forthcoming). The analysis of how they actually did it might also shed some light on the problems of misrepresentations.

How to Hide Words With Words

Only too often do we hear in public life that someone was quoted out of context, that their words were used out of context, that someone meant something else than what was reported by the media. The idea that users of language deceive others not only about reality around them is the second good thing about the book.

That trait was followed in the book in two ways. First, I attempted to formalize the concept of taking words out of context. Research into deception seems to disregard that people do not misrepresent only physical or social reality. People also misrepresent what others say and, again, not only what they say about extralinguistic reality but the way they say it. They misrepresent the function with which something is said. In other words, people ascribe to speakers goals different from those they might in fact have had, or that some conventional aspects of the utterance itself or features of the context suggested they had. To pinpoint what they are actually doing, I attempted to create the category of "taking words out of context" in the typology of deceptive strategies in Chapter 3.

The second way in which the idea of misrepresenting words was developed was in the notion of metadiscursive deception. People pretend that they are cooperative, whereas in fact they are not. Covert evasions, implicit misrepresentations, manipulation of felicity conditions, and probably a number of other strategies fall into the category.

Moreover, I have ended up with a neat distinction within deceptive strategies with respect to the object of misrepresentation. On the one hand, there are all those deceptions that misrepresent something else than the act of deception itself; on the other hand, there are all those that misrepresent the uncooperativeness of the utterance that is deceptive. In such a way, deception is construed as a communicative action covering the whole of reality.

Metadiscursive deception, finally, allows for communication to be incorporated more smoothly into the overall theory of deception. Linguistic deception is no different from its other forms and has the two main aspects—simulation (where the "extralinguistic deception" goes) and dissimulation (where its metadiscursive counterpart is located).

Conspiracy Theory

Deception, it seems, is at the core of noncooperation. A liar is normally viewed as doing something morally wrong. A liar can be sued and tried. A liar is someone who undermines the foundation on which human communication is built—the convention that we normally tell the truth, although in fact we deceive almost continually.

Deception, however, can be an act of cooperation. Interlocutors sharing a goal of trying to put a particular version of reality to their audience can team up and linguistically work together to misrepresent reality to serve their overall discursive goals.

The third good thing about the book is the idea of cooperating to be uncooperative. Cooperation has levels and degrees. A speaker aiming at deception, although uncooperative toward the target, may well be cooperating with another communicator in achieving the goal of deception. Furthermore, cooperation in misrepresenting reality may manifest itself both as an active contribution to it and as more passive acceptance of the other contributor's actions. This all, finally, is possible because deception in general and evasions, lies, or other deceptive strategies—unlike promises, questions, or apologies—are not associated with any conventional linguistic means carrying them. They are pragmatic acts. They are parasitic on other uses of language in the sense of speakers nonovertly using conventionally anchored speech acts to further their deceptive goals.

A LOOK BEYOND LANGUAGE

Multimodal Analysis

This book is about language and how it is used to deceive others. Deception, however, is not solely a linguistic domain. It can involve any symbolic activity of human beings. In what is left of this book, I take a brief look at what I think is a major complement of linguistic deception: deception by means of the visual.[1] I do so because I think that apart from possibly developing some categories discussed throughout the book, the major direction of deception research is to integrate the approach in the inquiries into linguistic and visual deception. I am not aware of any attempts at constructing a unified approach to different communicative modes of deception.

Yet calls for an integrated multimodal analysis of acts of communication, although perhaps still a relatively new development within the study of discourse, are already an established part of discourse analysis, particularly in its critical strand (see Kress, 1996; Kress, Leite-Garcia, & van Leeuwen, 1997; Kress & van Leeuwen, 1996). Advertisements, textbooks, newspapers, and television all not only communicate by linguistic means but also have a visual aspect that seems crucial to the message. Its analysis, therefore, is essential. Furthermore, analysts of the photographic message have long since pointed out that photographs are, as Barthes (1977) put it, a "floating chain of signifiers" (p. 39), and it is the linguistic message that, among other techniques, is a means of anchoring it. Benjamin, cited by Mitchell (1992), asks of captions whether they are not the essential components of pictures (see also Price & Wells, 1997). Although a recent analysis (Meinhof & Galasiński, forthcoming) showed a reverse relationship, that is, the photographic images anchoring personal narratives, the call for a multimodal analysis is all the stronger. It is also the photographic message that will be the main base of my discussion of deceptive possibilities of imagery.

Photography: An Exercise in Indexicality

In summer 1999, the British press was hit by another series of photographs of Diana, Princess of Wales. The event would not have been exceptional in its own right had it not been that some of the pictures presented scenes from Diana's family life—well, the family with her late companion, Dodi al Fayed. One of the photographs showed Diana and Dodi lovingly looking at their mixed-race child. The images, which came from the series Mental Images, by the photographer Alison Jackson, shown in London at the Blue Gallery, spurred a heated debate whether they are acceptable as art. They were, after all, so true!

Photographs are prone to being deceptive. The reason is their indexicality (e.g., Messaris, 1997): their documentary aspect. As Mitchell (1992) points out, a photograph can represent only something that exists in the physical world. A photograph always tells us that something that we can now find in the photograph was actually out there. This is precisely why advertisers attempt to pass paintings as photographs (see Key, 1989): Paintings do not carry the connotation of referring to reality. This is also why photographs are used as evidence (Mitchell, 1992), and this is where deception starts.

Indeed, Mitchell (1992) gives a number of examples in which the photographic message was, at the least, abused by those who claimed that they had evidence for what had happened. Ambassador Vernon Walters used dramatically blurred images of what he claimed to be armed Libyan planes as evidence of the justifiability of U.S. Navy fighters' action against them. The famous photograph of a Spanish soldier, taken by Robert Capa, apparently the instant the soldier was hit by the bullet that killed him, turned out to be a staged fake, as was another equally famous photograph of American soldiers hoisting a flag in Iwo Jima. Finally, Mitchell recalls a photograph apparently showing three Vietnam War pilots still surviving in a Vietnam camp. This time, the photograph turned out to be a doctored version of a 1923 photograph of three Russian farmers.

The rapidly developing computer technology added to the deceptive potential of photographs. Mitchell (1992; also Martin, 1991) reports that digital image manipulation was used by *National Geographic* when one of the magazine's photographs showed pyramids in Giza a bit closer to each other than they in fact are, but thus making a more exotic composition. In the same way, a celebrity can appear with his or her head "attached" to a different body, making in such a way a more attractive person.

Photographic Deception

Photographs tell us that things shown on them exist. There are, however, a number of ways in which the photographic image can be manipulated to mislead its audience. Messaris (1997) and Mitchell (1992) offer different, although slightly overlapping, accounts of how photographs can be deceptive. Messaris's typology is predominantly based on how a photograph can deceive by representing something that did happen. Mitchell, on the other hand, is mainly interested in how photographs show something that in fact did not happen. Although the former is interested in the manipulation of the photograph itself, the latter deals with what the photograph denotes.

Messaris (1997) lists three main ways in which the photographic image can be manipulated: staging, editing, and selection. He also adds mislabeling, that is, false representation of what the photograph represents (see also Price, 1997), and altering (a category that roughly subsumes the categories proposed by Mitchell, 1992). Messaris's typology refers to cases in which photographs actually have denotation in physical reality. They are deceptive in how they show it. *Staging* occurs when the photograph is presented as if it had represented an unmanipulated reality. It pretends to show reality as taking its natural course without human (the photographer's) intervention. *Editing,* on the other hand, shows a number of events linked together, for example, in a cause-effect relationship, or, simply, in a chronological relationship as happening one after the other. Editing pertains particularly to the realms of moving images: news reports, documentaries, and advertising. Messaris's example refers to the impression of a seamless children's ball game that in fact was continually interrupted by its relative difficulty. Its smoothness, and thus potential ease and attractiveness, was implied by editing. Finally, *selection* in image manipulation refers to the control of what is shown to the addressee. An unrepresentative photograph in a series, yet shown as typical, could be misleading. On the other hand, what is left out of an image, for example, by cropping or framing, is a way of exercising control of what the viewer will see as a representation of a state of affairs.

Messaris's (1997) account of photographic deception is founded on the assumption of the photograph's indexicality. What the image refers to did happen. Indeed, in all three cases, the photographs show an actual state of affairs. Deceptiveness of those photographs lies in the pretense that they are straightforward photographs, that they show what they are assumed to show: reality of which the photographer was a mere observer, the one who merely looks at what is to be photographed (Barthes, 1993).

Alternatively, Mitchell (1992) focuses on techniques of image manipulation, mentioning four types. *Insertions* are additions of elements to the photographic image that had not been part of the photographed scene. The state of affairs denoted is "enriched" by an additional element. In such a way, a photograph of a single plane can become a photograph of a number of aircraft in formation. *Effacement* and *elisions* are the opposite of insertions. This time, an element is eliminated from the photographed scene. Mitchell shows how the technique is used for political ends when politically inconvenient people are removed from a picture—the reality represented is sanitized, never including undesirable elements. When Oprah Winfrey is shown with a body that does not belong to her, says Mitchell, we are dealing with a *substitution,* a technique that enables the deceiver to replace one element with another one of the type. Finally, *anachronistic assemblages* are not merely attempts at "correcting" or "sanitizing" reality—they are attempts at showing things that have not happened. In this case, people who never met could be shown, for example, in a meeting—a misrepresentation with potentially disastrous consequences in political life.

In his typology, Mitchell (1992) attempted to lay out the possibilities of how photographs can show reality that never was. The photograph is not merely abused, as we could claim in Messaris's typology; this time, the assumption of iconicity (the photograph is normally assumed to be an icon of—to resemble—what it stands for) is violated. There is no referent of the photograph.

Of course, the techniques described by Mitchell (1992) do not have to be used with deceptive goals but can be used with interesting effect, for example, in cinema. The idea behind films such as Barry Levinson's *Wag the Dog* focuses precisely on the notion of photographic deception. Although *Wag the Dog* was a film about media manipulation, the digital manipulation of archive footage used in, say, *Forrest Gump* (directed by Robert Zemeckis), was simply part of the film narrative.

Extralinguistic Versus Metadiscursive Deception in Photography

If one of the aims of research into deceptive activities of human beings is to provide a common framework for different modes by which people can deceive others, then it seems that linguistic deception, as described throughout the book, and photographic deception share one significant characteristic. The two typologies of visual deception discussed above not only show two ways in which photographs can deceive but also provide a distinction between two types of photographic deception with regard to its object. Mitchell (1992) and Messaris (1997) in fact describe what in linguistic terms I have called *extralinguistic* and *metadiscursive* deception, respectively.

Mitchell (1992) shows how a photograph creates a false reality. It either falsifies it (as in anachronistic assemblages) or distorts it, as in, for example, effacements. Messaris (1997), in contrast, shows how a photograph that is—shall I say—uncooperative pretends to be cooperative. Messaris's typology refers to techniques in which the photographic message pretends to be unaltered, pretends to be straightforwardly indexical. Deceptiveness of staging, editing, and selection is metadiscursive. The attempts of the sender are to misrepresent the photograph itself.

Messaris (1997) proposes that photographic images have two semantic features: iconicity and indexicality—they resemble what they stand for, and what they stand for does exist in the photographed reality, respectively. I suggest that the photographic equivalent of extralinguistic deception (Mitchell's typology) is a violation of the assumption of iconicity. What the photograph shows is not similar to what in fact happened. The photograph does not resemble anything that happened in reality.

The photographic equivalent of metadiscursive deception (Messaris's typology) is a violation of the assumption of the photograph's indexicality. Here, what the photograph shows did actually happen—the photograph is an icon of something that happened—it resembles reality. What it shows, however, did not happen in the way the photograph suggests. There is not a straightforward indexical relationship between the image and the fact.

Producing forgeries is also an exercise in metadiscursive deception. Although the perfect fake might be identical with the original, still the original has the history of production that is required to create the original of the work. The forgery only pretends to have it (for a more detailed discussion of the status of forgeries, see Goodman, 1976). On the other hand, paintings posing as photographs (see Key, 1989) are both extralinguistic and metadiscursive. Paintings are not iconic—they are creations of a painter—but by posing to be photographs, they are also metadiscursive; they pretend to be indexical.

There is just one other category in Messaris's (1997) typology that I have not yet discussed. Mislabeling of photographs consists of claiming that what the photograph shows is something different from what it in fact is. It seems that the category belongs with photographs that are deceptive "extralinguistically," that is, they misrepresent something else than themselves. A mislabeled photograph does not pretend to be cooperative while being uncooperative. Although the state of affairs a mislabeled photograph represents does exist, it seems that the goal of the photograph is to violate the assumption of iconicity. In other words, there is a hiatus between what the photograph shows and what it says it shows: The caption constructs the photograph as misrepresenting physical reality. What the photograph is said to represent in fact does not look like that at all.

This brief account of photographic deception suggests that the broad framework of deception in language also seems to work with regard to visual communication, or at least an aspect of it. It suggests, further, the potential need to investigate to what extent this distinction within deception works also for other areas within the visual mode, or indeed within other types of deception.

FINAL WORD

I started this book by saying that although humans are driven by truth bias, deception in human relations is not only abundant but also normal. Although the high moral ground is always likely to tell us that lying (once again putting it as a stereotypical act of deceptive communication) is bad, it seems that the presence of deception in our everyday life is at least ambiguous. Deception, it seems, is, at least according to Aitchison (1996), an indispensable part of humanity. And, if we, human beings, did not have deception, I could not write a book about it.

Furthermore, there are not many acts that can be as heroic as an act of deception. The heroic lie (cf. Tischner, 1982)—an act of deception committed by a victim of repression, an act of not betraying comrades, an act of fooling the enemy—can be an act of utmost bravery.

Tischner (1990) also argues that every lie contains a homage to truth, necessary be it to preserve the liar's credibility. A liar must lie coherently, otherwise he or she will give the game away. The rules of the truth of coherence are indispensable also for the liar her- or himself. The act of lying, continues Tischner, implies the value of truth in three ways: It confirms the target's expectation of truth; it also affirms that the lie, to be successful, must pass itself as truth; and, finally, a liar must abide by the rules of the truth by coherence.

Would therefore deception be the best friend of truthfulness? I do not know the answer to that question. I do know, however, that deception has been with us for a long time. It is still here and will be universally present in our lives for at least the foreseeable future. It also seems that it is not such a bad thing, after all! Trust me, I'm a doctor.

NOTE

1. By the visual, I mean images that are different from, say, facial expressions or gestures or other nonverbal behaviors and actions. Nonverbal communication has received a lot of attention in deception research (e.g., Miller & Stiff, 1993), especially with regard to leakage of deceptive actions. Here, I am interested in images external to the human body.

References

Adams, T. D. (1990). *Telling lies in modern American autobiography.* Chapel Hill: University of North Carolina Press.

Aitchison, J. (1996). *The seeds of speech: Language origin and evolution.* Cambridge, UK: Cambridge University Press.

Anderson, M. (1986). Cultural concatenation of deceit and secrecy. In R. W. Mitchell & N. S. Thompson (Eds.), *Deception: Perspectives on human and non-human deceit* (pp. 323-348). New York: State University of New York Press.

Austin, J. L. (1962). *How to do things with words.* Oxford, UK: Oxford University Press.

Bailey, F. G. (1988). *Humbuggery and manipulation: The art of leadership.* Ithaca, NY: Cornell University Press.

Bailey, F. G. (1991). *The prevalence of deceit.* Ithaca, NY: Cornell University Press.

Barnes, J. (1994). *A pack of lies.* Cambridge, UK: Cambridge University Press.

Barthes, R. (1977). *Image—music—text.* London: Fontana.

Barthes, R. (1993). *Camera lucida.* London: Vintage.

Basso, E. B. (1987). *In favor of deceit: A study of tricksters in an Amazonian society.* Tucson: University of Arizona Press.

Bavelas, J. B., Black, A., Chovil, N., & Mullett, J. (1990a). *Equivocal communication.* Newbury Park, CA: Sage.

Bavelas, J. B., Black, A., Chovil, N., & Mullett, J. (1990b). Truths, lies, and equivocations: The effects of conflicting goals on discourse. *Journal of Language and Social Psychology, 9,* 135-161.

Bell, A. (1991). *The language of news media.* Oxford, UK: Blackwell.

Bell, D. M. (1997). Innuendo. *Journal of Pragmatics, 27,* 35-59.

Benoit, W. L., & Wells, W. T. (1996). *Candidates in conflict.* Tuscaloosa: University of Alabama Press.

Billig, M. (1995). *Banal nationalism.* London: Sage.

Bilmes, J. (n.d.). Misinformation in verbal accounts: Some fundamental considerations. *Man (N.S.), 10,* 60-71.

Blum-Kulka, S. (1997). Discourse pragmatics. In T. A. van Dijk (Ed.), *Discourse as social interaction* (pp. 38-63). London: Sage.

Bok, S. (1978). *Lying.* Hassocks, UK: Harvester Press.

Bok, S. (1982). *Secrets.* New York: Pantheon.

Bolinger, D. (1973). Truth is a linguistic question. *Language, 49,* 539-550.

Bourdieu, P. (1991). *Language and symbolic power.* Cambridge, MA: Polity.

Bowers, J. W., Elliot, N. D., & Desmond, R. J. (1977, Spring). Exploiting pragmatic rules: Devious messages. *Human Communication Research, 3*(3), 235-242.

Bradac, J. (1983). The language of lovers, flowers and friends: Communicating in social and personal relationships. *Journal of Language and Social Psychology, 2,* 141-162.

Bradac, J., Friedman, E., & Giles, H. (1986). A social approach to propositional communication: Speakers lie to hearers. In G. McGregor (Ed.), *Language for hearers* (pp. 127-151). Oxford, UK: Pergamon.

Broad, W., & Wade, N. (1982). *Betrayers of truth.* New York: Simon & Schuster.

Brown, G., & Yule, G. (1983). *Discourse analysis.* Cambridge, UK: Cambridge University Press.

Brown, P., & Levinson, S. (1987). *Politeness.* Cambridge, UK: Cambridge University Press.

Bull, P. (1994). On identifying questions, replies and non-replies in political interviews. *Journal of Language and Social Psychology, 13,* 115-131.

Bull, P. (1997). Queen of hearts or queen of the arts of implication? *Social Psychological Review, 1,* 27-36.

Bull, P., & Mayer, K. (1993). How not to answer questions in political interviews. *Political Psychology, 14,* 651-666.

Buller, D. B., & Burgoon, J. K. (1994). Deception: Strategic and non-strategic communication. In J. A. Daly & J. M. Wiemann (Eds.), *Strategic interpersonal communication* (pp. 191-223). Hillsdale, NJ: Lawrence Erlbaum.

Buller, D. B., & Burgoon, J. K. (1996a). Another look at information management: A rejoinder to McCornack, Levine, Morrison, and Lapinski. *Communication Monographs, 63,* 92-98.

Buller, D. B., & Burgoon, J. K. (1996b). Interpersonal deception theory. *Communication Theory, 6,* 203-242.

Burgoon, J. K., & Buller, D. B. (1996). Reflections on the nature of theory building and the theoretical status of interpersonal deception theory. *Communication Theory, 6,* 311-328.

Burgoon, J. K., Buller, D. B., Ebesu, A. S., White, C. H., & Rockwell, P. A. (1996). Testing interpersonal deception theory: Effects of suspicion on communication behaviors and perceptions. *Communication Theory, 6,* 243-267.

Burgoon, J. K., Buller, D. B., Guerrero, L. K., Afifi, W. A., & Feldman, C. M. (1996). Interpersonal deception: XII. Information management dimensions underlying deceptive and truthful messages. *Communication Monographs, 63,* 50-69.

Burgoon, M., Callister, M., & Hunsaker, F. G. (1994, July). *Patients who deceive: An empirical investigation of patient-physician communication.* Paper presented at the 5th International Conference on Language and Social Psychology, University of Queensland, Brisbane, Australia.

Burgoon, M., Hunsaker, F. G., & Dawson E. J. (1994). *Human communication.* Thousand Oaks, CA: Sage.

Burke, R. R., DeSarbo, W. S., Oliver, R. L., & Robertson, T. S. (1988). Deception by implication: Experimental investigation. *Journal of Consumer Research, 14,* 483-494.

Bursten, B. (1973). *The manipulator.* New Haven, CT: Yale University Press.

Caldas-Coulthard, R. C., & Coulthard, M. (Eds.). (1996). *Texts and practices.* London: Routledge.

Castelfranchi, C., & Poggi, I. (1994). Lying as pretending to give information. In H. Parret (Ed.), *Pretending to communicate* (pp. 276-291). Berlin, Germany: Walter de Gruyter.

Chilton, P., & Schaeffner, C. (1997). Discourse and politics. In T. A. van Dijk (Ed.), *Discourse as social interaction* (pp. 206-230). London: Sage.

Chisholm, R. M., & Feehan, T. D. (1977). The intent to deceive. *Journal of Philosophy, 74,* 143-159.

Chouliaraki, L., & Fairclough, N. (1999). *Discourse in late modernity: Renewing critical discourse analysis.* Edinburgh, UK: Edinburgh University Press.

Chovil, N. (1994). Equivocation as an interactional event. In W. R. Cupach & B. H. Spitzberg (Eds.), *The dark side of interpersonal communication* (pp. 105-123). Hillsdale, NJ: Lawrence Erlbaum.

Cialdini, R. (1985). *Influence: Science and practice.* Glenview, IL: Scott, Foresman.

Clark, H. H. (1987). Four dimensions of language use. In J. J. Verschueren & M. Bertucelli-Papi (Eds.), *The pragmatic perspective* (pp. 9-25). Amsterdam: John Benjamins.

Clark, H. H., & Carlson, T. (1982). Hearers and speech acts. *Language, 58,* 332-373.

Cody, M., & McLaughlin, M. L. (Eds.). (1990). *The psychology of tactical communication.* London: Multilingual Matters.

Coleman, L., & Kay, P. (1981). Prototype semantics: The English word *lie. Language, 57*(1), 26-44.

Cook, G. (1989). *Discourse.* Oxford, UK: Oxford University Press.

Daniel, D. C., & Herbig, K. L. (1982a). Propositions on military deception. In D. C. Daniel & K. L. Herbig (Eds.), *Strategic military deception* (pp. 3-30). New York: Pergamon.

Daniel, D. C., & Herbig, K. L. (Eds.). (1982b). *Strategic military deception.* New York: Pergamon.

Dascal, M. (1977). Conversational relevance. *Journal of Pragmatics, 1,* 309-328.

Delumeau, J. (1994). *Grzech i strach* [Sin and fear]. Warsaw, Poland: Instytut Wydawniczy PAX. (Original work published 1983 as *La peche et la peur*)

DePaulo, B. M. (1988). Non-verbal aspects of deception. *Journal of Non-Verbal Behavior, 12,* 153-162.

DePaulo, B. M., Ansfield, M. E., & Bell, K. L. (1996). Theories about deception and paradigms for studying it: A critical appraisal of Buller and Burgoon's interpersonal deception theory and research. *Communication Theory, 6,* 297-310.

Dillon, J. T. (1990). *The practice of questioning.* London: Routledge.

Ekman, P. (1985). *Telling lies: Clues to deceit in the marketplace, politics, and marriage.* New York: Norton.

Ekman, P. (1988). Lying and non-verbal behavior: Theoretical issues and new findings. *Journal of Non-Verbal Behavior, 12,* 163-176.

Eliade, M. (1966). *Traktat o historii religii* [Polish translation of Treaty on the origins of religions]. Warsaw, Poland: Ksiazka i Wiedza.

Englehardt, E. E., & Evans, D. (1994). Lies, deception and public relations. *Public Relations Review, 20,* 249-266.

Epstein, J. J. (1982). The grammar of a lie: Its legal implications. In R. J. Di Pietro (Ed.), *Linguistics and the professions* (pp. 133-142). Norwood, NJ: Ablex.

Fairclough, N. (1989). *Language and power.* London: Longman.

Fairclough, N. (1992). *Discourse and social change.* Oxford, UK: Polity.

Fairclough, N. (1995). *Media discourse.* London: Edward Arnold.

Fowler, R. (1991). *Language in the news.* London: Routledge.

Fowler, R., Hodge, B., Kress, G., & Trew, T. (Eds.). (1979). *Language and control.* London: Routledge.

Fraser, B. (1994). No conversation without misrepresentation. In H. Parret (Ed.), *Pretending to communicate* (pp. 143-153). Berlin, Germany: Walter de Gruyter.

Galasiński, D. (1992). *Chwalenie się jako perswazyjny akt mowy* [Boasting as a persuasive speech act]. Kraków, Poland: Instytut Języka Polskiego PAN.

Galasiński, D. (1994a, July). *Conceptualising deception.* Paper presented at the 44th annual conference of the ICA, Sydney, Australia.

Galasiński, D. (1994b). Czy przestrzeganie regul konwersacyjnych zawsze sprzyja udatności aktu mowy? [Is following of the conversational rules always conducive to the success of the speech act?]. *Polonica, 16,* 69-83.

Galasiński, D. (1996a). Deceptiveness of evasion. *Text, 16,* 1-22.

Galasiński, D. (1996b). Pretending to cooperate: How speakers hide evasive actions. *Argumentation, 10,* 375-388.

Galasiński, D. (1998). Strategies of talking to each other: Rule breaking in Polish presidential debates. *Journal of Language and Social Psychology, 17*(2), 165-182.

Galasiński, D. (forthcoming). "Sensationally frank revelations." Metalinguistic constructions of extralinguistic reality in the coverage of the Princess Diana interview.

Garfinkel, A. (1977). Truths, half-truths and deception. *Papers in Linguistics, 10,* 135-149.

Geis, M. L. (1982). *The language of television advertising.* New York: Academic Press.

Gibbons, P., Bradac, J. J., & Busch, J. D. (1992). The role of language in negotiations: Threats and promises. In L. L. Putnam & M. E. Roloff (Eds.), *Communication and negotiation* (pp. 156-175). Newbury Park, CA: Sage.

Gilsenan, M. (1976). Lying, honor and contradiction. In B. Kapferer (Ed.), *Transaction and meaning* (pp. 191-219). Philadelphia: Institute for the Study of Human Issues.

Giora, R. (1994). On the political message: Pretending to communicate. In H. Parret (Ed.), *Pretending to communicate* (pp. 105-123). Berlin, Germany: Walter de Gruyter.

Goffman, E. (1969). *Strategic interaction.* Philadelphia: University of Pennsylvania Press.

Goffman, E. (1986). *Frame analysis.* Boston: Northeastern University Press.

Goffman, E. (1990). *Stigma.* London: Penguin.

Goodin, R. E. (1980). *Manipulatory politics.* New Haven, CT: Yale University Press.

Goodman, N. (1976). *Languages of art.* Indianapolis, IN: Hackett.

Gorayska, B., & Lindsay, R. (1993). The roots of relevance. *Journal of Pragmatics, 19,* 301-323.

Graesser, A. C., & Franklin, S. P. (1990). QUEST: A cognitive model of question answering. *Discourse Processes, 13,* 279-303.

Grice, H. P. (1975). Logic and conversation. In P. Cole & J. Morgan (Eds.), *Speech acts* (Syntax and Semantics, Vol. 3, pp. 41-58). New York: Academic Press.

Grice, H. P. (1981). Presupposition and conversational implicature. In P. Cole (Ed.), *Radical pragmatics* (pp. 183-198). New York: Academic Press.

Grice, H. P. (1989). *Study in the way of words.* Cambridge, MA: Harvard University Press.

Gruber, H. (1993). Political language and textual vagueness. *Pragmatics, 3,* 1-28.

Grzegorczykowa, R. (1990). *Wprowadzenie do semantyki językoznawczej* [Introduction to linguistic semantics]. Warsaw, Poland: Państwowe Wydawnictwo Naukowe.

Guriewicz, A. (1987). *Problemy średniowiecznej kultury ludowej* [Problems of medieval folk culture]. Warsaw, Poland: Państwowy Instytut Wydawniczy.

Habermas, J. (1979). *Communication and the evolution of society.* London: Heinemann.

Habermas, J. (1987). *The theory of communicative action* (Vol. 2). Cambridge, MA: Polity.

Halliday, M. A. K. (1978). *Language as social semiotic.* London: Edward Arnold.

Halliday, M. A. K. (1994). *An introduction to functional grammar* (2nd ed.). London: Edward Arnold.

Halliday, M. A. K., & Hasan, R. (1985). *Language, context, and text.* Oxford, UK: Oxford University Press.

Hall-Jamieson, K. (1992). *Dirty politics.* New York: Oxford University Press.

Hamilton, M. A., & Mineo, P. J. (1998). A framework for understanding equivocation. *Journal in Language and Social Psychology, 17,* 3-35.

Handel, M. (1982). Intelligence and deception. *Journal of Strategic Studies, 5*(1), 122-154.

Harder, P., & Kock, C. (1976). *The theory of presupposition failure.* Copenhagen, Denmark: Akademisk Forlag.

Harris, S. (1991). Evasive action: How politicians respond to questions in political interviews. In P. Scannell (Ed.), *Broadcast talk* (pp. 76-99). London: Sage.

Hitchcock, D. (1992). Relevance. *Argumentation, 6*(2), 251-270.

Hodge, R., & Kress, G. (1993). *Language as ideology.* London: Routledge.

Holdcroft, D. (1987). Conversational relevance. In J. J. Verschueren & M. Bertucelli-Papi (Eds.), *The pragmatic perspective* (pp. 477-495). Amsterdam: John Benjamins.

Hopper, R., & Bell, R. A. (1984). Broadening the deception construct. *Quarterly Journal of Speech, 70,* 288-302.

Howard, M. (1992). *Strategic deception in the Second World War.* London: Pimlico.

Jacobs, S., Dawson, E. J., & Brashers, D. (1996). Information manipulation theory: A replication and assessment. *Communication Monographs, 63,* 70-82.

Jacobs, S., Brashers, D., & Dawson, E. J. (1996). Truth and deception. *Communication Monographs, 63,* 98-103.

Jakobson, R. (1960). Closing statement: Linguistics and poetics. In T. Sebeok (Ed.), *Style in language* (pp. 350-377). Cambridge: MIT Press.

Jaworski, A. (1993). *The power of silence: Social and pragmatic perspectives*. London: Sage.

Kalbfleisch, P. J. (1994). The language of detecting deceit. *Journal of Language and Social Psychology, 13,* 469-496.

Kaluża, I. (1990). *The language of deception in Macbeth.* Kraków, Poland: Uniwersytet Jagiellonski.

Kassin, S. M., Williams, L. N., & Saunders, C. L. (1990). Dirty tricks of cross-examination. *Law and Human Behavior, 14,* 373-384.

Kazimierski, J. (1996). Kłamstwo jako diagnoza i klamstwo jako metoda (Dostojewski, Solżenicyn, Wat.) [Lie as a diagnosis and lie as a method (Dostoyevsky, Solzhenitsin, Wat)]. In Z. Wójcicka & P. Urbański (Eds.), *Klamstwo w literaturze* [Lie in literature] (pp. 211-220). Kielce, Poland: Wydawnictwo Szumacher.

Key, W. B. (1989). *The age of manipulation.* Lanham, MD: Madison.

Kłoskowska, A. (1996). *Kultury narodowe u korzeni* [National cultures at their roots]. Warsaw, Poland: Wydawnictwo Naukowe PWN.

Knapp, M. L., & Comadena, M. F. (1979). Telling like it isn't: A review of theory and research on deceptive communication. *Human Communication Research, 5,* 270-285.

Knapp, M. L., & Vangelisti, A. L. (1992). *Interpersonal communication and human relationships.* Boston: Allyn & Bacon.

Kress, G. (1991). Critical discourse analysis. *Annual Review of Applied Linguistics, 11,* 84-99.

Kress, G. (1996). Representational resources and the production of subjectivity. In C. R. Caldas-Coulthard & M. Coulthard (Eds.), *Texts and practices* (15-31). London: Routledge.

Kress, G., Leite-Garcia, R., & van Leeuwen, T. (1997). Discourse semiotics. In T. van Dijk (Ed.), *Discourse as structure and process* (pp. 257-291). London: Sage.

Kress, G., & van Leeuwen, T. (1996). *Reading images.* London: Routledge.

Kreuz, R. J., & Graesser, A. C. (1993). The assumptions behind questions in letters to advice columnists. *Text, 13*(1), 65-89.

Leech, G. N. (1983). *Principles of pragmatics.* London: Longman.

Levinson, S. (1983). *Pragmatics.* Cambridge, UK: Cambridge University Press.

Lévi-Strauss, C. (1963). *Structural anthropology.* New York: Basic Books.

Lewicki, R. (1983). Lying and deception. In M. Bazermann & R. Lewicki (Eds.), *Negotiating in organizations* (pp. 68-90). Beverly Hills, CA: Sage.

Lewis, D. K. (1969). *Convention.* Cambridge, MA: Harvard University Press.

Lieberman, B. (1977). Deception and collective action. *Philosophica, 20*(2), 65-84.

Lippard, P. V. (1988). "Ask me no questions, I'll tell you no lies": Situational exigencies for interpersonal deception. *Western Journal of Speech Communication, 52,* 91-103.

Loftus, E. F. (1975). Leading questions and the eyewitness report. *Cognitive Psychology, 7,* 560-572.

Martin, E. (1991). On photographic manipulation. *Journal of Mass Media Ethics, 6,* 156-163.

Martin, L. J. (1982). Disinformation: An instrumentality in the propaganda arsenal. *Political Communication and Persuasion, 2,* 47-64.

Mawby, R., & Mitchell, R. W. (1986). Feints and ruses: An analysis of deception in sports. In R. W. Mitchell & N. S. Thompson (Eds.), *Deception: Perspectives on human and non-human deceit* (pp. 313-322). New York: State University of New York Press.

McCornack, S. A. (1992). Information manipulation theory. *Communication Monographs, 59,* 1-16.

McCornack, S. A. (1997). The generation of deceptive messages: Laying groundwork for a viable theory of interpersonal deception. In J. O. Greene (Ed.), *Message production advances in communication theory* (pp. 91-126). Hillsdale, NJ: Lawrence Erlbaum.

McCornack, S. A., Levine, T. R., Morrison, K., & Lapinski, M. (1996). Speaking of information manipulation: A critical rejoinder. *Communication Monographs, 63,* 83-92.

McLaughlin, M. (1984). *Conversation: How talk is organized.* Beverly Hills, CA: Sage.

Meinhof, U. H., & Galasiński, D. (forthcoming). Photography, memory, and the construction of identities on the former East-West German border.

Messaris, P. (1997). *Visual persuasion.* Thousand Oaks, CA: Sage.

Metts, S. (1989). An exploratory investigation of deception in close relationships. *Journal of Social and Personal Relationships, 6,* 159-179.

Mey, J. L. (1993). *Pragmatics.* Oxford, UK: Blackwell.

Millar, K. U., & Tesser, A. (1988). Deceptive behavior in social relationships: A consequence of violated expectations. *Journal of Psychology, 122,* 263-273.

Miller, G. (1983). Telling it like it isn't and not telling it like it is: Some thoughts on deceptive communication. In J. I. Sisco (Ed.), *The Jensen lectures: Contemporary communication studies* (pp. 91-116). Tampa: University of South Florida.

Miller, G., deTurck, M. A., & Kalbfleisch, P. J. (1983). Self-monitoring, rehearsal and deceptive communication. *Human Communication Research, 10,* 97-117.

Miller, G., Mongeau, P. A., & Sleight, C. (1986). Fudging with friends and lying to lovers: Deceptive communication in personal relationships. *Journal of Social and Personal Relationships, 3,* 495-512.

Miller, G., & Stiff, J. B. (1993). *Deceptive communication.* Newbury Park, CA: Sage.

Mitchell, R. W. (1986). A framework for discussing deception. In R. W. Mitchell & N. S. Thompson (Eds.), *Deception: Perspectives on human and non-human deceit* (pp. 1-39). New York: State University of New York Press.

Mitchell, W. J. (1992). *The reconfigured eye.* Cambridge: MIT Press.

Moose, P. H. (1982). A systems view of deception. In D. C. Daniel & K. L. Herbig (Eds.), *Strategic military deception* (pp. 136-150). New York: Pergamon.

Mura, S. S. (1983). Licensing violations: Legitimate violation of Grice's conversational principle. In R. T. Craig & K. Tracy (Eds.), *Conversational coherence: Form, structure and strategy* (pp. 101-115). Beverly Hills, CA: Sage.

Naughton, J. M., & Craig, R. (1994, July). *A clash over formulation in a televised interview.* Paper presented at the 5th International Conference on Language and Social Psychology, University of Queensland, Brisbane, Australia.

Nawrocka, E. (1996). O czym kłamia i dlaczego historycy literatury? [What do historians of literature lie about and why?]. In Z. Wójcicka & P. Urbański (Eds.), *Kłamstwo w literaturze* [Lie in literature] (pp. 141-150). Kielce, Poland: Wydawnictwo Szumacher.

Ng, S. H., & Bradac, J. J. (1993). *Power in language*. Newbury Park, CA: Sage.

Nuyts, J (1989). On the functionality of language. *IPrA Papers in Pragmatics, 3*(1), 88-129.

Nyberg, D. (1993). *The varnished truth: Truth telling and deceiving in ordinary life.* Chicago: University of Chicago Press.

O'Hair, D., & Friedrich, G. W. (1992). *Strategic communication in business and the professions*. Boston: Houghton Mifflin.

O'Hair, H. D., & Cody, M. J. (1994). Deception. In W. R. Cupach & B. H. Spitzberg (Eds.), *The dark side of interpersonal communication* (pp. 181-213). Hillsdale, NJ: Lawrence Erlbaum.

O'Hair, H. D., Cody, M. J., & McLaughlin, M. L. (1981). Prepared lies, spontaneous lies, Machiavellianism and non-verbal communication. *Human Communication Research, 7,* 325-339.

Orr, C. J., & Burkins, K. E. (1976). The endorsement of evasive leaders: An exploratory study. *Central States Speech Journal, 62,* 230-239.

Parret, H. (Ed.). (1994). *Pretending to communicate*. Berlin, Germany: Walter de Gruyter.

Perry, J. A. G. (n.d.). Land, power and the lie. *Man (N.S.), 16,* 235-250.

Peters, G. M. (1987). The use of lies in negotiation. *Ohio State Law Journal, 48,* 1-50.

Pisarkowa, K. (1986). O komunikatywnej funkcji przemilczenia [On the communicative function of being silent about]. *Zeszyty Prasoznawcze, 29*(1), 25-34.

Preston, I. L. (1994). *The tangled web they weave: Truth, falsity and advertisers.* Madison: University of Wisconsin Press.

Price, D. (1997). Surveyors and surveyed. In L. Wells (Ed.), *Photography: A critical introduction* (pp. 55-102). London: Routledge.

Price, D., & Wells, L. (1997). Thinking about photography. In L. Wells (Ed.), *Photography: A critical introduction* (pp. 11-54). London: Routledge.

Puzynina, J. (1992). *Język w świecie wartości* [Language in the world of values]. Warsaw, Poland: Państwowe Wydawnictwo Naukowe.

Reboul, A. (1994). The description of lies in speech act theory. In H. Parret (Ed.), *Pretending to communicate* (pp. 292-298). Berlin, Germany: Walter de Gruyter.

Reece, B. B., & Ducoffe, R. H. (1987). Deception in brand names. *Journal of Public Policy and Marketing, 6,* 93-103.

Richards, J. I. (1990). *Deceptive advertising.* Hillsdale, NJ: Lawrence Erlbaum.

Roberts, J. M., & Nutini, H. G. (1988). Witchcraft event staging in rural Tlaxcala: A study in inferred deception. *Ethnology, 27,* 407-431.

Robinson, W. P. (1993). Lying in the public domain. *American Behavioral Scientist, 36,* 359-382.

Robinson, W. P. (1994). Reactions to falsifications in public and interpersonal contexts. *Journal of Language and Social Psychology, 13,* 497-513.

Robinson, W. P. (1996). *Deceit, delusion, and detection.* Thousand Oaks, CA: Sage.

Rudinow, J. (1978). Manipulation, *Ethics, 88,* 338-347.

Sanders, R. E. (1987). *Cognitive foundations of calculated speech.* New York: State University of New York Press.

Sarangi, S. K., & Slembrouck, S. (1992). Non-cooperation in communication: A reassessment of Gricean pragmatics. *Journal of Pragmatics, 17,* 117-154.

Sarangi, S. K., & Slembrouck, S. (1996). *Language, bureaucracy and social control.* London: Longman.

Schiffrin, D. (1994). *Approaches to discourse.* Oxford, UK: Blackwell.

Searle, J. R. (1969). *Speech acts.* Cambridge, UK: Cambridge University Press.

Searle, J. R. (1975). Indirect speech acts. In P. Cole & J. L. Morgan (Eds.), *Speech acts* (Syntax and Semantics, Vol. 3, pp. 59-82). New York: Academic Press.

Searle, J. R. (1979). *Expression and meaning.* Cambridge, UK: Cambridge University Press.

Sexton, D. J. (1986). The theory and psychology of military deception. In R. W. Mitchell & N. S. Thompson (Eds.), *Deception: Perspectives on human and non-human deceit* (pp. 349-356). New York: State University of New York Press.

Shibles, W. (1988). A revision of the definition of lying as an untruth told with intent to deceive. *Argumentation, 2,* 99-115.

Shuy, R. W. (1993). *Language crimes.* Oxford, UK: Blackwell.

Shuy, R. W. (1998). *The language of confession, interrogation, and deception.* Thousand Oaks, CA: Sage.

Simpson, P. (1993). *Language, ideology and point of view.* London: Routledge.

Sluzki, C. E., Beavin, J., Tarnopolsky, A., & Veron, E. (1967). Transactional disqualification: Research on the double bind. *Archives of General Psychiatry, 16,* 494-504.

Stebbins, R. A. (1975). Putting people on: Deception of our fellowman in everyday life. *Sociology and Social Research, 59,* 189-200.

Stiff, J. B. (1995). Conceptualising deception as a persuasive activity. In C. R. Berger & M. Burgoon (Eds.), *Communication and social influence process* (pp. 73-90). East Lansing: Michigan State University Press.

Stiff, J. B. (1996). Theoretical approaches to the study of deceptive communication: Comments on interpersonal deception theory. *Communication Theory, 6,* 289-296.

Stiff, J. B., & Miller, G. R. (1986). "Come to think of it...": Interrogative probes, deceptive communication, and deception detection. *Human Communication Research, 12,* 339-357.

Stomma, L. (1986). *Antrolopogia wsi polskiej XIX wieku* [Anthropology of the Polish village of the 19th century]. Warsaw, Poland: Instytut Wydawniczy PAX.

Su, S. P. (1994). *Lexical ambiguity in poetry.* London: Longman

Sweetser, E. E. (1987). The definition of *lie.* In D. Holland & N. Quinn (Eds.), *Cultural models in language and thought* (pp. 3-66). Cambridge, UK: Cambridge University Press.

Tanaka, K. (1994). *Advertising language.* London: Routledge.

Thomas, J. (1995). *Meaning in interaction.* London: Longman.

Tischner, J. (1982). *Myślenie według wartości* [Thinking according to values]. Kraków, Poland: Znak.

Tischner, J. (1990). *Filozofia dramatu* [Philosophy of drama]. Paris: Kultura.

Trosborg, A. (1997). Contracts as social action. In B.-L. Gunnarsson, P. Linell, & B. Nordberg (Eds.), *The construction of professional discourse* (pp. 55-75). London: Longman.

Tuchman, B. W. (1993). *Odległe zwierciadło* [Polish translation of A distant mirror]. Katowice, Poland: Wydawnictwo "Ksiażnica."

Turner, R. E., Edgley, C., & Olmstead, G. (1975). Information control in conversations: Honesty is not always the best policy. *Kansas Journal of Sociology, 11,* 69-89.

van der Meij, H. (1987). Assumptions of information-seeking questions. *Questioning Exchange, 1,* 111-118.

van Dijk, T. A. (1991). Principles of critical discourse analysis. *Discourse and Society, 4,* 249-283.

van Dijk, T. A. (1997). The study of discourse. In T. A. van Dijk (Ed.), *Discourse as structure and process* (pp. 1-34). London: Sage.

Verschueren, J. (1985). *What people say they do with words.* Norwood, NJ: Ablex.

Vincent, J. M., & Castelfranchi, C. (1981). On the art of deception. In H. Parret, M. Sbisa, & J. Verschueren (Eds.), *Possibilities and limitations of pragmatics* (pp. 749-777). Amsterdam: John Benjamins.

Walton, D. (1995). *A pragmatic theory of fallacy.* Tuscaloosa: University of Alabama Press.

Watzlawick, P. (1976). *How real is real.* New York: Random House.

Weaver, P. H. (1994). *News and the culture of lying.* New York: Free Press.

Whaley, B. (1982). Toward a general theory of deception. *Journal of Strategic Studies, 5,* 178-192.

Whiten, A., & Byrne, R. W. (1988). Tactical deception in primates. *Behavioral and Brain Sciences, 11,* 233-244.

Wilson, J. (1990). *Politically speaking.* Oxford, UK: Basil Blackwell.

Wilson, J. (1991). The linguistic pragmatics of terrorist acts. *Discourse and Society, 2,* 29-45.

Zadrożyńska, A. (1988). *Powtarzać czas od początku* [To start the time anew] (Vol. 2). Warsaw, Poland: Wydawnictwo spóldzielcze.

Zagorin, P. (1990). *Ways of lying.* Cambridge, MA: Harvard University Press.

Zuckerman, M., DePaulo, B., & Rosenthal, R. (1981). Verbal and non-verbal communication of deception. In L. Berkowitz (Ed.), *Advances in experimental psychology* (Vol. 14, pp. 1-59). New York: Academic Press.

Author Index

Subject Index

[illegible stamp]

UNIVERSITY OF WOLVERHAMPTON
LEARNING RESOURCES

About the Author

Dariusz Galasiński is Reader in Media and Cultural Studies at the University of Wolverhampton, United Kingdom. He received his doctorate from the Jagiellonian University, Kraków, Poland. His dissertation, on pragmatic aspects of boasting, was published as a book in 1992. His main interests and most of his published work focus on the problems of strategic and deceptive communication and discursive representation. His recent major projects include research into media representations of middle age (funded by the Leverhulme Trust, UK) and identities in border communities in Europe (funded by the Economic and Social Research Council, UK, and the European Commission).